CHILTERN WALKS

HERTFORDSHIRE, BEDFORDSHIRE & NORTH BUCKINGHAMSHIRE

Nick Moon

This book is one of a series of three, which provide a comprehensive coverage of walks throughout the whole of the Chiltern area (as defined by the Chiltern Society). The walks included vary in length from 2.1 to 11.1 miles, but are mainly in the 5- to 7-mile range popular for half-day walks, although suggestions for possible combinations of walks are given for those preferring a full day's walk.

Each walk gives details of nearby places of interest and is accompanied by a specially drawn map of the route which also indicates local pubs and a skeleton road network.

The author, Nick Moon, has lived in or regularly visited the Chilterns all his life and has, for over 30 years, been an active member of the Chiltern Society's Rights of Way Group, which seeks to protect and improve the area's footpath and bridleway network. Thanks to the help and encouragement of the late Don Gresswell MBE, he was introduced to the writing of books of walks and has since written or contributed to a number of publications in this field.

OTHER PUBLICATIONS BY NICK MOON

Chiltern Walks Trilogy
Chiltern Walks 1 : Hertfordshire, Bedfordshire and North
        Buckinghamshire:
        Book Castle (new edition) 2007
Chiltern Walks 2 : Buckinghamshire :
        Book Castle (new edition) 2005
Chiltern Walks 3 : Oxfordshire and West Buckinghamshire :
        Book Castle (new edition) 2001

Circular Walks along the Chiltern Way
Volume 1 :   Buckinghamshire and Oxfordshire
        Book Castle 2004
Volume 2 :   Hertfordshire and Bedfordshire
        Book Castle 2005

Family Walks
Family Walks 1 : Chilterns - South : Book Castle 1997
Family Walks 2 : Chilterns - North : Book Castle 1998

The Chiltern Way & Chiltern Way Extensions
        Book Castle (expanded edition) 2003

Oxfordshire Walks
Oxfordshire Walks 1: Oxford, the Cotswolds and the Cherwell Valley
        Book Castle (new edition) 1998
Oxfordshire Walks 2: Oxford, the Downs and the Thames Valley
        Book Castle (new edition) 2001

The D'Arcy Dalton Way across the Oxfordshire Cotswolds and
        Thames Valley : Book Castle 1999

First published April 1993
New edition 2007
by The Book Castle 12 Church Street, Dunstable, Bedfordshire

@ Nick Moon, 2007

Printed in Great Britain by Antony Rowe Ltd., Chippenham, Wilts.

ISBN 978 1 903747 87 2

Contents

POSSIBLE LONGER WALKS PRODUCED BY COMBINING WALKS DESCRIBED IN THE BOOK

Walks	Miles	Km	Walks	Miles	Km
2A + 3	13.2	21.2	14A + 15	16.9	27.2
2A + 3 + 4A	19.6	31.5	14C + 15	13.1	21.0
2A + 4A	13.3	21.4	17 + 18A	13.1	21.1
2A + 4A + 5	20.8	33.4	19 + 20	14.4	23.1
2B + 3	12.1	19.4	21A + 22	15.0	24.1
2B + 3 + 4B	17.9	28.8	23 + 24	13.7	22.0
2B + 4B	11.6	18.7	23 + 24 + 25	21.9	35.2
2B + 4B + 5	19.1	30.7	23 + 24 + 26A	22.0	35.4
4A + 5	13.9	22.3	23 + 24 + 26B	15.6	25.1
4B + 5	13.3	21.4	23 + 25	15.3	24.7
7A + 8	16.7	26.9	23 + 25 + 26A	20.6 or 23.9	33.1 or 38.5
7A + 14A	16.9	27.2	23 + 25 + 26B	17.6	28.3
7A + 14B	14.3	23.0	24 + 25 + 26B	17.5	28.2
7B + 8	11.0	17.6	25 + 26A	13.1 or 16.4	21.1 or 26.5
7C + 14A	14.2	22.8	25 + 26B	10.1	16.3
7C + 14B	11.6	18.6	26A + 27	15.7	25.2
9 + 12A	13.6	22.0	26A + 28	17.1	27.6
9 + 12A + 13	21.5	34.5	26C + 27	13.7	22.1
9 + 12B	12.7	20.5	26C + 27 + 28	21.3	34.3
9 + 12B + 13	20.6	33.1	26C + 28	15.1	24.3
9 + 13	14.8	23.8	27 + 28	14.2	22.8
13 + 17	12.6	20.2	27 + 28 + 29	21.4	34.5
13 + 17 + 18A	19.3	31.1	28 + 29	14.7	23.7

Cover Photograph: View from Highpark Wood looking towards Water End. (Walk 7).

© Nick Moon.

Introduction

This book of walks is one of three covering the whole of the Chilterns from the Goring Gap on the River Thames to the Hitchin Gap in North Hertfordshire. The area covered by this volume includes the whole of the Hertfordshire and Bedfordshire Chilterns as well as the detached part of the Buckinghamshire Chilterns north of Tring. From a geographical point of view, the county boundaries in this area have no logical basis and in practice the area covered by this book, which offers the walker a great variety of attractive countryside to explore, is divided into two distinct parts both by its natural geography and the influence of man, the dividing line being the M1 and Luton and Dunstable conurbation. To the southwest of this line, the hills are traversed by the River Colne and its tributaries, the Ver, Gade, Bulbourne and Chess, which flow southwards to join the Thames in Staines to the west of London, whereas to the northeast of it, the River Lea, which rises in Luton, and its tributary, the Mimram flow southeastwards to join the Thames in East London and in the extreme northeast corner, the Hiz and its tributaries, the Oughton and the Purwell, flow northwards into the Ouse.

Within this area to the north and east of Luton, the escarpment, here known as the Barton Hills, includes some of the finest and yet least known downland in the Chilterns, while the interior is dominated by Lilley Bottom, a wide valley resembling Hampden Bottom in Bucks, which becomes the Mimram valley above Whitwell. The hills to the northeast of this valley traversed by a maze of narrow lanes are quiet and well-wooded and so are most inviting for the walker to explore. To the southwest a more open ridge gradually giving way to the gentle rolling hills of Central Hertfordshire separates Lilley Bottom from Luton and the Lea valley.

South of the Luton conurbation, the first ridge separating the Lea and Ver valleys and climbing to the lofty heights of Blow's Down is generally open in nature and has suffered somewhat from insensitive development. The next ridge, however, between the Ver and Gade valleys, dropping gently from the mighty Dunstable Downs to Hemel Hempstead and the M1, and the Gade valley above Hemel have been largely spared the scourge of modern development and with their scattering of woods and remote rural atmosphere offer an expanse of fine walking country. Between the Gade and Bulbourne valleys is a ridge dominated by the Ashridge Estate, which rises to the Ivinghoe Hills and, with its mixture of copious woodland, picturesque villages and lofty downs is probably the most popular walking area in this book. South of the Bulbourne valley, where the Grand Union Canal

5

towpath and Tring Reservoirs provide pleasant waterside walks, is a range of hills straddled by the Bucks. boundary and the Chess valley, probably the most attractive valley in the northern Chilterns, while finally to the south of Rickmansworth, the Colne valley and hills on the former Middlesex border offer surprisingly rural walks with fine views within twenty miles of Central London.

The majority of walks included in this book are in the 5-7 mile range, which is justifiably popular for half-day walks, but, for the less energetic or for short winter afternoons, a few shorter versions are indicated in the text, while others can be devised with the assistance of a map. In addition, a number of walks in the 7-11 mile range are included for those preferring a leisurely day´s walk or for longer spring and summer afternoons, while a list of possible combinations of walks is provided for those favouring a full day´s walk of up to 23 miles.

Details of how to reach the starting points by car are given in the introductory information to each walk and any convenient railway stations are shown on the accompanying plan. Current information on bus routes and operators can be obtained by telephoning the hotline on 0870-608 2608.

All the walks described here follow public rights of way, use recognised permissive paths or cross public open space. As the majority of walks cross land used for economic purposes such as agriculture, forestry or the rearing of game, walkers are urged to follow the Country Code at all times:

• Be **safe** - plan ahead and follow any signs.
• **Leave** gates and property as you find them.
• **Protect** plants and animals, and take your litter home.
• Keep dogs under close **control**.
• **Consider** other people.

Observing these rules helps prevent financial loss to landowners and damage to the environment, as well as the all-too-frequent and sometimes justified bad feeling towards walkers in the countryside.

While it is hoped that the special maps provided with each walk will assist the user to complete the walks without going astray and skeleton details of the surrounding road network are given to enable walkers to shorten the routes in emergency, it is always advisable to take an Ordnance Survey or Chiltern Society map with you to enable you to shorten or otherwise vary the routes without using roads or get your bearings if you do become seriously lost. Details of the appropriate maps are given in the introductory information of each walk.

As for other equipment, readers are advised that some mud will

6

normally be encountered on most walks particularly in woodland except in the driest weather. However proper walking boots are to be recommended at all times as, even when there are no mud problems, hard ruts or rough surfaces make the protection given by boots to the ankles desirable. In addition, the nature of the countryside makes many Chiltern paths prone to overgrowth, particularly in summer. To avoid resultant discomfort, protective clothing is advisable, especially where specific warnings are given.

Some of the walks may already be familiar to readers as they were previously published in 'Walks in the Hertfordshire Chilterns' or 'Walks for Motorists : Chilterns (Northern Area)' which are now out of print, but more than half are completely new or have been radically altered, while all of the old walks have been rechecked and brought up to date. In addition, as the walks are appearing in the Chiltern Society's name, all the path numbers have been shown on the plans and incorporated into the texts. These numbers, which are also shown on the Society's Footpath Maps (where available), consist of the official County Council footpath number with the prefix letters used by the Society to indicate the parish concerned. It is therefore most helpful to use these when reporting any path problems you may find, together, if possible, with the national grid reference for the precise location of the trouble spot, as, in this way, the problem can be identified on the ground with a minimum of loss of time in looking for it. National grid references can, however, only be calculated with the help of Ordnance Survey Landranger or Explorer maps and an explanation of how this is done can be found in the Key to each map.

The length of time required for any particular walk depends on a number of factors such as your personal walking speed, the number of hills, stiles, etc. to be negotiated, whether or not you stop to rest, eat or drink, investigate places of interest, etc. and the number of impediments such as mud, crops, overgrowth, ploughing, etc. which you encounter, but generally an average speed of between two and two and a half miles per hour is about right in the Chilterns. It is, however, always advisable to allow extra time if you are limited by the daylight or catching a particular bus or train home in order to avoid your walk developing into a race against the clock. Should you have problems with any of the paths used on the walks or find that the description given is no longer correct, the author would be most grateful if you could let him have details (c/o The Book Castle), so that attempts can be made to rectify the problem or the text can be corrected at the next reprint. Nevertheless, the author hopes that you will not encounter any serious problems and have pleasure from following the walks.

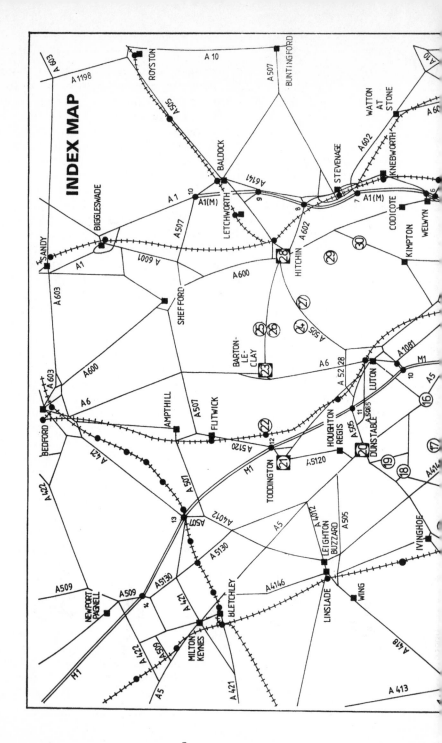

8

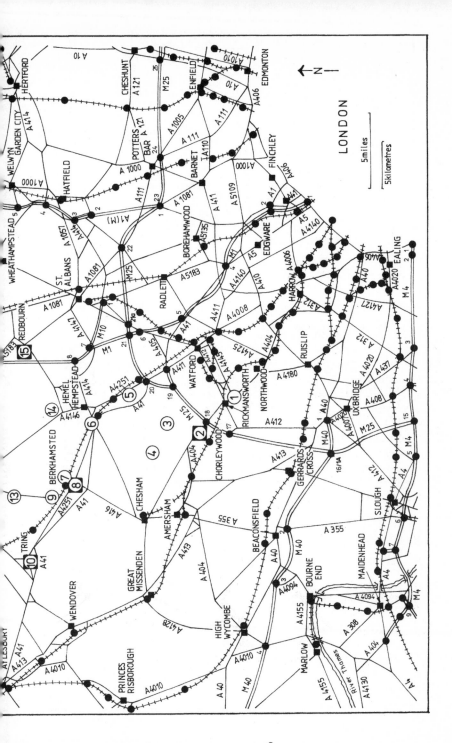

9

The Chiltern Society was founded in 1965 with the objects: "To encourage high standards of town and country planning and architecture and to stimulate public interest in and care for the beauty, history and character of the area of the Chiltern Hills." The Society Rights of Way Group actively protects and restores public rights of way in the Chilterns - some 5,000 paths. It has surveyed every individual path and takes up irregularities with local parish councils, district or county councils to preserve public rights. It organises voluntary working parties most weeks to clear, waymark or otherwise encourage the use of paths for the public to enjoy the Chiltern countryside. Details of the Society's activities and footpath maps as well as membership application forms can be obtained from the Chiltern Society Office:

The Chiltern Society
White Hill Centre
White Hill
Chesham
Buckinghamshire HP5 1AG

Tel. No. : 01494 771250
E-mail   : office@chilternsociety.org.uk
Website   : www.chilternsociety.org.uk

WALK 1:   Rickmansworth (Batchworth)

Length of Walk: 7.1 miles / 11.4 Km
Starting Point: Roundabout at the junction of the A404 and A4145 at Batchworth on the edge of Rickmansworth.
Grid Ref: TQO64939
Maps: OS Landranger Sheet 176
OS Explorer Sheet 172
(part only) Chiltern Society FP Map No.28
Parking: Cars can be parked in the service road alongside the A4145 (Moor Lane) at its junction with the A404. Access to this service road can be obtained from the roundabout.

Rickmansworth, familiarly known as 'Ricky', is situated at the confluence of three Chiltern rivers, the Colne, the Gade and the Chess. These waterways together with the presence of two ancient parks close to the town have ensured that its setting has remained relatively rural despite the rapid expansion which resulted from the coming of the Metropolitan Line in 1887. Indeed if one visits the old town centre with its narrow streets, which through-traffic now bypasses, it still retains its quiet country town atmosphere, even if the genuine old buildings have been supplemented by a number of modern imitations. The parish church, which was largely rebuilt in 1826 and 1890, retains its old tower dating from 1630 and a number of old brasses and monuments including the tomb of Sir Robert Carey, first Earl of Monmouth, who in 1603 rode to Holyrood to inform King James VI of Scotland of the death of Queen Elizabeth I and his consequent succession to the English throne. Other famous names associated with the town include Cardinal Wolsey, who owned Moor Park, William Penn, the prominent Quaker and founder of Pennsylvania, who lived at Basing House in the 1670s and the writer, George Eliot, who also lived in the town.

The walk, which is of a fairly easy nature, soon leaves the town behind and follows the Grand Union Canal towpath in its surprisingly rural setting to Springwell Lock before crossing the canal and continuing parallel to it to the edge of Harefield. It then climbs through a bluebell wood to Hill End and crosses the hills to Woodcock Hill and Batchworth Heath with fine views at a number

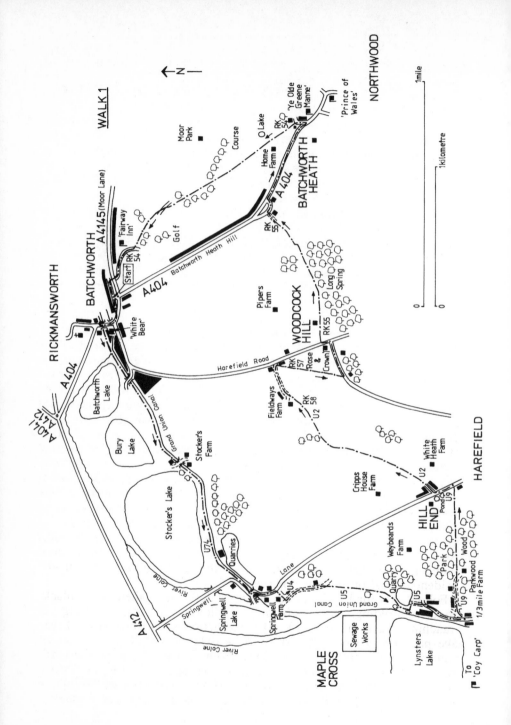

WALK 1

of points, before returning across Moor Park Golf Course with its splendid mansion to your point of departure.

Starting from the roundabout at the junction of the A404 and A4145 at Batchworth on the edge of Rickmansworth, follow the right-hand pavement of the A404 towards Rickmansworth for some 300 yards. After passing the 'White Bear' and crossing the bridge over the Grand Union Canal, turn right down a flight of steps to reach the canal towpath at Batchworth Lock. Here turn right passing under the A404 bridge and following the towpath straight on, soon leaving the town behind. After three-quarters of a mile, on reaching Stocker's Lock, to your left is Stocker's Farm which became famous as the set for the TV series of 'Black Beauty'. Just past the lock, go under a hump-backed bridge and continue to follow the towpath (later on path U74) for a further two-thirds of a mile, at one point passing a large boundary stone marking the boundary of Hertfordshire and the former county of Middlesex and then a derelict cement works.

At Springwell Lock leave the towpath and join Springwell Lane to your right. Just past the lock follow the road turning left over Bridge No.176, then turning right and climbing gently past a number of cottages. Having passed the cottages, at a sharp left-hand bend where a right-hand crash-barrier ends, fork right into a fenced lane (path U4) passing an electronic gate. On nearing a barn, fork left into a rough lane and follow it gently uphill with wide views across the Colne valley towards the distant M25 opening out to your right. On reaching some farm buildings, keep left at a fork, then, where the track bears left, leave it and take path U5 straight on between fences to a bridlegate. Now follow a right-hand fence, later a hedge, to the far end of the field. Here go through the right-hand of three gates and take a hedged path straight on to a gate at the edge of woodland. Go through this gate, then turn right onto a fenced path downhill, soon with an old quarry to your left, to reach another gate. Now take a fenced path through scrubland between the quarry and the canal bank eventually reaching the quarry entrance. Here turn right into Summerhouse Lane, soon reaching the end of a macadamed residential road on the edge of Harefield.

Follow this road straight on for over 300 yards, then, by a black wooden building, turn left into Bellevue Terrace, ignoring a branching track to your left. At the junction with Barrington Drive, take path U9, a rough access road, straight on uphill passing some cottages. At the entrance to Parkwood Farm Kennels, leave the road and go straight on between anti-horse barriers into a fenced path which climbs through Park Wood, in early May a mass of bluebells. At the top of the hill, cross a footbridge over a spring, then take the fenced path straight on between fields to a road at Hill End.

Cross this road and turn left along its pavement, then, opposite a large pond concealed by willow trees, turn right into Plough Lane (path U2), an access road to a number of houses. At the far end of this road go straight on over a stile into a field, then bear slightly left following a depression in the ground across the field heading just left of a distant copse to cross a footbridge and stiles. Here bear slightly left and follow a left-hand hedge. Where the hedge bears left, leave it and go straight on to cross a stile under a tree in a corner of the field. Now follow a left-hand hedge straight on downhill to a stile and footbridge, then follow a crop break straight on uphill to a hedge gap at the county boundary. Here take path RK58 beside a left-hand hedge to Fieldways Farm where you join the farm drive and follow it straight on. Just before reaching Harefield Road, turn sharp right over a stile onto path RK57 crossing a field diagonally to pass just left of an electricity pole and cross a stile just left of the far corner of the field. Now bear half right across the corner of the next field to a gap in the right-hand hedge, then cross a further field diagonally to a stile in the far corner leading to Harefield Road opposite a county boundary stone.

Turn left onto this road, then, at a road junction by the 'Rose and Crown' at Woodcock Hill, turn left. Opposite the pub car park turn right onto fenced path RK55. Where this emerges into a field with fine views ahead towards Batchworth Heath, go straight on downhill to a hedge gap in the bottom corner, then follow the outside edge of a wood called Long Spring downhill. At the bottom of the hill, leave the right-hand hedge and go straight on across the field to pass a redundant stile step in the far corner. Now turn right and follow a right-hand hedge along the edge of a golf course, ignoring a gap in the hedge, then looking out for a wooden fence to your right. Here fork right between bollards into a green lane leading to a layby on the A404 at Batchworth Heath Hill. Turn right into the layby and where it ends, cross the A404, turn right onto its pavement and follow it downhill and up again to Batchworth Heath.

At the top of the hill turn left into Park Close. Where the road turns right, leave it and take enclosed path RK54 straight on between private drives, soon emerging onto Moor Park Golf Course. Here go straight on, following a series of four-foot wooden marker posts with white arrows passing left of a small lake and crossing several fairways. Having traversed a small copse, there is a fine view to your right of Moor Park mansion. Described by Sir Niklaus Pevsner as 'the grandest eighteenth-century mansion in Hertfordshire', Moor Park is, in fact, a seventeenth-century house which was remodelled in the Palladian style for the merchant Benjamin Styles by the architect Sir

James Thornhill between 1725 and 1727 with a rich rococo interior and a large classical portico. The house, which had, before its remodelling, been the home of the ill-fated Duke of Monmouth, was acquired by Rickmansworth UDC in 1937 and is now almost certainly the most magnificent golf clubhouse in the country.

Continue to follow the marker posts straight on, passing a bench, then right of a copse, then left of a second copse to join a macadam drive by a gnarled oak tree. Follow this drive for about 50 yards then fork right, following the marker posts diagonally across a fairway, then bearing slightly left to pass through a gap in a tree belt and continue downhill to rejoin the macadam drive. Turn right onto this and follow it past the 'Fairway Inn' and on to the A4145. Cross this road carefully, then turn left for your starting point.

WALK 2:   Chorleywood

Length of Walk: (A) 6.9 miles / 11.1 Km
                    (B) 5.8 miles / 9.3 Km
Starting Point: Car park on south side of A404 by
                     Chorleywood Cricket Pavilion.
Grid Ref: TQ034967
Maps: OS Landranger Sheets 166 or 176
            OS Explorer Sheet 172
            Chiltern Society FP Map No.28
How to get there / Parking: Chorleywood, 2 miles northwest
    of Rickmansworth, may be reached by leaving the M25 at
    Junction 18 and taking the A404 towards Amersham.
    Having passed Chorleywood Church on your left, the car
    park by the cricket pavilion is some 300 yards beyond on
    your left.
Notes: Heavy nettle growth may be encountered at several points
    on both walks in the summer months, while bridleway CN3
    is prone to deep mud in places, even in dry weather.

Chorleywood, with its 200-acre partially wooded common, is
perhaps a typical example of the curious mixture of countryside and
suburbia found in what was once called `Metroland` . To the east
and west of the common are sizeable built-up areas which have
grown up since the Metropolitan Railway reached the village in
1889, while the spacious common itself is surrounded by typical
Chiltern cottages and on the edge of the village is the farmhouse
where the Quaker, William Penn, who later founded the American
state of Pennsylvania, was married in 1672.
    Both walks first lead you across the common to the built-up area
around Chorleywood Station before leaving the village and passing
through pleasant beechwoods and a long green lane to the outskirts
of Chenies. Here Walk B leads you through the village before
dropping into the Chess valley at Sarratt Bottom, while Walk A
makes a gradual and scenic descent into the Chess valley at the
picture-book village of Latimer. It then turns to follow the Chess
valley downstream past the ruins of the old Flaunden Church as
well as Dodds Mill to rejoin Walk B. Both walks then climb to
Sarratt Church before returning across the Chess valley and
through Chorleywood Park to your starting point.

16

Both walks start from the car park by Chorleywood Cricket Pavilion on the south side of the A404 and take path CW32b, a wide glade leading from the rear of the car park across the wooded common. On emerging from the trees, go straight on until you reach a worn crossing path. Turn left onto this path and follow it, ignoring a fork to the left at one point, until you reach Common Road at a gap in the houses by a bus stop left of the 'Rose and Crown'. Cross the road here and take path CW15, a macadam lane called Colley Land, straight on downhill. This later narrows to a path and reaches another road by the Metropolitan Line embankment. Turn right onto this road then immediately left under a railway bridge. At a crossroads by a shopping parade, turn right and at a fork, go right again into the continuation of Whitelands Avenue. Ignore two branching roads to the left, then between 59 and 61 Whitelands Avenue, turn left onto fenced path CW39 passing through a squeeze-stile and taking the path into Carpenter's Wood.

On reaching the wood, turn immediately right and follow back garden fences along the edge of the wood. Where the gardens end, go straight on through Whitelands Wood, soon walking parallel to and later joining a permissive bridleway. At the far side of the wood turn right onto bridleway CN3 joining the Chiltern Way and passing either side of a gate then under a railway bridge. Now in Buckinghamshire, take a hedged, stone-based lane straight on for over half a mile, passing through Halsey's Wood and eventually reaching the A404 at Chenies Turn. Here cross the A404 and leaving the Chiltern Way, turn left onto its pavement, following it for some 200 yards, then turn right onto path CN34, the rough drive to Great House Farm, with wide views of the Chess valley to your left and of Chenies Manor House, rebuilt by the first Earl of Bedford in 1530, and the outskirts of the village to your right.

On reaching a fork, **Walk B** turns right onto bridleway CN35 and follows this, then the village street, straight on to the picturesque village green. Here, at a fork, leave the road and bear slightly right across the green passing between the bus shelter and well (built in 1977 to celebrate the Queen's Silver Jubilee) and crossing two roads to enter a macadam lane left of a white cottage with lattice windows where you join **Walk 4A**. Now see the text of **Walk 4**.

At the junction of CN34/CN35, **Walk 2A** takes bridleway CN35 straight on to the start of a left-hand copse. Here turn left onto path CN48, the drive to 'The Farm House', then immediately turn right over a low rail-stile. Now follow an obvious path through the copse to a stile. Cross this, a farm road and another stile opposite and take path CN42 straight on through a wood. At a fork bear left to cross a stile at the edge of the wood with a fine view of Latimer nestling in the Chess

17

valley ahead. Here turn right over a second stile, then turn left and gradually diverge from the left-hand fence to cross a further stile. Now take a fenced path straight on to reach the top corner of Coney Wood, then follow the top edge of this wood, later a right-hand hedge to enter a corner of Walk Wood. Just inside the wood, turn right over a stile where you obtain a fine view of Latimer and the Chess valley with Latimer House partially hidden in trees on the wooded hill to your left.

Latimer, until the nineteenth century variously known as 'Isenhampstead Cheynduit` or 'Isenhampstead Latimer`, was formerly a hamlet of Chesham belonging to the Cavendish family (later the Lords Chesham) of Latimer House. The original house, where Charles I was held prisoner in 1647, was largely rebuilt in the nineteenth century in neo-Tudor style. The village church was also rebuilt in 1841 and renovated by Sir George Gilbert Scott in 1867, while many of the picturesque village cottages also date from this period.

Now bear half left across the field to a stile in the bottom left-hand corner leading to a crossroads. Cross the stile and the major road and take the road signposted to Latimer and Flaunden straight on to a bridge over the River Chess by a weir. At the far end of the bridge, turn right over a stile left of a green gate onto path LT20 following a right-hand fence at first, then bearing slightly right across the field to cross a culvert. Now keep straight on across the next field to reach a bend in the River Chess, then take bridleway CN56, bearing slightly left across the field to the left-hand corner of a copse concealing the ruins of the old Flaunden church. This thirteenth-century church was abandoned in 1838 when a new church was built in the hilltop village of Flaunden more than a mile away. Although the old church was still used for occasional services, it was already a ruin by the late nineteenth century and very little of it now remains. Here follow its fence straight on to a gate, then turn left across the field to a gate in the top fence. Do **not** go through this, but turn right and follow a left-hand fence through two fields passing an old tomb surrounded by iron railings. At the far end of the second field, ignoring a footpath and bridleway to your left, go straight on through a gate and take an enclosed bridleway beside an arm of the River Chess to Mill Farm at Chenies Bottom, then go straight on through the farmyard to a road near Dodds Mill.

Walks 2A and 4B turn left onto the road and follow it to a left-hand bend. Here leave the road and take path CN60 straight on over a stile by a gate then follow a right-hand fence to the far end of the field. Here cross a stile and go straight on across the next field to a stile into Limeshill Wood in the far corner of the field. Now, back in Hertfordshire, take path SA37 straight on through the wood then take

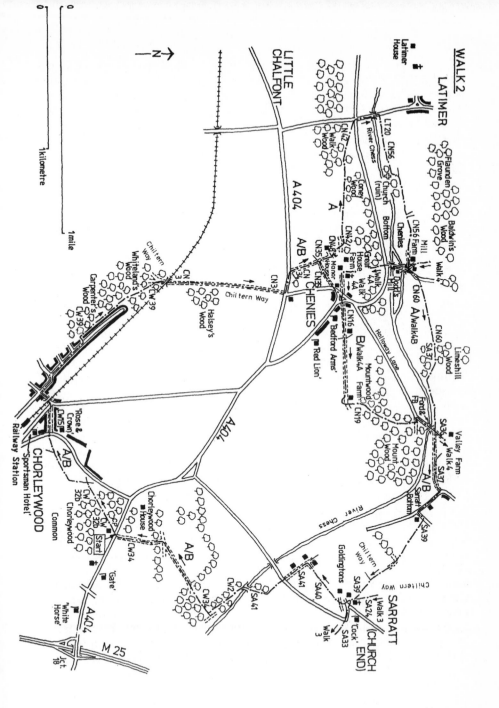

WALK 2

LATIMER

LITTLE CHALFONT

Latimer House

A 404

CHENIES

CHORLEYWOOD

SARRATT (CHURCH END)

Chorleywood Common

"Sportsman Hotel"
Railway Station

'Rose & Crown'

'White Horse'

'Gate'

'Red Lion'

'Bedford Arms'

M 25

Jct. 18

N →

0   1 kilometre

0   1 mile

Chiltern Way

River Chess

a fenced path, soon bearing right then left and later crossing a stile. Eventually you pass through a squeeze-stile leading to a junction of concrete and tarmac roads by a ford and footbridge over the Chess, where **Walk 4B** turns left onto path SA36 rejoining **Walk 4A** (now return to the text of **Walk 4**), while **Walk 2A** takes path SA37 straight on rejoining **Walk 2B**.

Walks 2A and 2B now follow the concrete road straight on for a quarter mile to a bend in a road by some cottages at Sarratt Bottom. Turn right onto this road and at a junction turn left past a white cottage. Some 50 yards beyond the cottage, turn right through a kissing-gate onto path SA39 and follow a right-hand hedge to a stile. Cross this and bear slightly left across a field to the far left-hand corner. Here ignore a stile to your left and bear slightly right into a tree-lined lane, following this uphill. Near the top, take the Chiltern Way straight on over a stile by a gate into a field and follow its right-hand hedge. At the far side of the field, leaving the Chiltern Way, bear half right over a stile and through a kissing-gate into Sarratt churchyard (briefly joining **Walk 3**) and take a gravel path passing right of the twelfth-century church (described in the introduction to Walk 3).

At a fork in the path, go right (leaving **Walk 3** again), passing through a gap in the churchyard wall and turning right through a kissing-gate onto path SA40 soon reaching the macadam drive to an early nineteenth-century manor house called Goldingtons. Cross this drive and a stile, with a fine view of the Chess valley ahead, and follow a right-hand fence straight on downhill to cross a stile near a cottage and join its drive. Now follow this, turning left onto path SA41 to reach a road. Cross this and go through a kissing-gate opposite, then follow a right-hand hedge straight on to the far end of the field. Here turn right into a thicket and follow a left-hand fence beside a poplar copse to a floodwalk leading to a footbridge over a very picturesque section of the River Chess. Just beyond the end of this footbridge, turn left through a kissing-gate onto path CW2 into a belt of trees. Disregarding a fork to the left, take an obvious path straight on for about 350 yards to a T-junction of paths at the far end of the tree-belt. Here turn right onto path CW34 into a wood and follow a well-defined path uphill, eventually joining a track which soon enters an avenue of chestnut trees in Chorleywood Park. Follow this avenue to its far end, then at a junction of tracks, turn right. On reaching a macadam drive, turn left onto it and follow it, with Chorleywood House soon coming into view to your right, until you reach gates leading to the A404 directly opposite your starting point.

WALK 3:   Sarratt

Length of Walk: 6.3 miles / 10.1 Km
Starting Point: 'The Boot`, Sarratt Green.
Grid Ref: TQO42996
Maps: OS Landranger Sheets 166 or 176
              OS Explorer Sheet 172
              Chiltern Society FP Maps Nos. 5 & 28
How to get there / Parking: Sarratt Green, 3.5 miles north of
     Rickmansworth, may be reached by leaving the M25 at
     Junction 18 and taking the A404 towards Amersham. After
     1 mile turn right onto a road signposted to Sarratt and follow
     it for 1.6 miles to a crossroads near the 'Cricketers` at Sarratt
     Green. Here turn left and find a suitable parking space along
     the quiet service road on the left side of the village green.
Notes: Heavy nettle growth may be encountered at several points
     in the summer months and part of path SA24 is prone to
     deep mud even in dry weather.

Sarratt, despite its close proximity to the M25 and the large built-up
areas of Watford and Rickmansworth, has a remarkably rural
setting. The traditional Chiltern cottages of what is now the main
village at Sarratt Green are ranged around an attractive and
unusually long green with a duckpond at one end, while the ancient
village known as Church End about two-thirds of a mile away on
the northern slopes of the Chess valley now has little more than the
church, a pub, a nineteenth-century manor house and some
almshouses rebuilt in the same period. The cruciform twelfth-
century church, appropriately dedicated to the Holy Cross, is
particularly interesting as its tower was rebuilt in the fifteenth
century in part with Roman bricks (presumably emanating from
the ruins of a Roman villa discovered in the vicinity) and it is also
the only church tower in Hertfordshire to have a saddleback roof.
The church, restored by Sir George Gilbert Scott in 1865, also
contains a Norman font, a fragment of a thirteenth-century wall-
painting and a carved Jacobean pulpit, from which the renowned
Nonconformist Richard Baxter preached in the seventeenth century.
    The walk, which explores the surprisingly remote hilltop plateau
between Watford and the Chess valley with its bluebell woods, leads
you from Sarratt Green via the wooded Dawes Common to Church

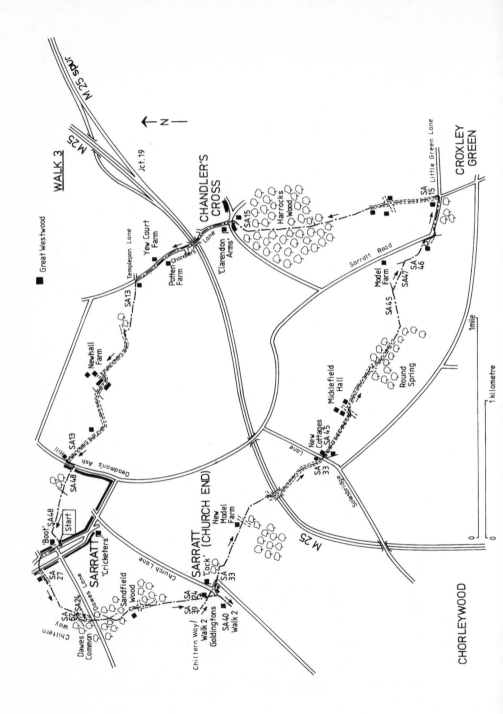

WALK 3

N

■ Great Westwood

CHANDLER'S CROSS

SARRATT

SARRATT (CHURCH END)

CROXLEY GREEN

CHORLEYWOOD

M 25 spur

M25

Jct. 19

Yew Court Farm

Templepan Lane

Potten Chandlers Lane Farm

'Clarendon Arms'

SA15

Harrocks Wood

Little Green Lane

SA 15

Sarratt Road

Model Farm

SA47

SA 46

SA13

Newhall Farm

SA13

Deadman's Ash Hill

Mickelfield Hall

Round Spring

SA45

New Cottages SA 45

Lane

SA48

'Boot' SA48

Start

'Cricketers'

SA 27

Church Lane

'Cock'

SA 33

New Model Farm

SA 33

Solesbridge Lane

M 25

1 mile

1 kilometre

Sandfield Wood

SA 39 SA 24

SA 40 Walk 2

Chiltern Way / Walk 2 Goldingtons

SA 25 SA24

Dawes Lane

SA Chiltern Dawes Way Common

22

End, near which fine views open out from time to time across the Chess Valley. It then takes you over the M25 and via Micklefield Hall to the edge of Croxley Green, before returning by way of Chandler's Cross to Sarratt Green.

Starting from the 'Boot' pub on the northeast side of Sarratt Green, take the road along the edge of the green northwestwards to its junction with the road to Commonwood, then bear half left across the green, passing left of a pond to reach a path signposted to Dawes Common (SA27). Take this path along a gravel lane, ignoring branching drives to your right, to cross a stile by a gate at the far end. Now bear slightly right across a field to the corner of a hedge ahead, then follow the left-hand hedge until it turns left. Here bear half left across the field to cross a stile in the field corner into the wooded Dawes Common. In the wood at a three-way fork, take the right-hand option (path SA52), then, at a further junction, take the second path to your left (SA24) joining the Chiltern Way. At a fork keep left, soon passing a green metal seat to your left, then ignore a crossing horse track and soon reach Dawes Lane.

Cross this road and go through a kissing-gate by a gate opposite and take path SA24 straight on, following a right-hand fence through woodland, then ignoring a branching path to your left and becoming enclosed by a second fence. After a quarter mile, having passed a house to your right, you emerge onto its drive and keep straight on along it. At a left-hand bend fork right through a kissing-gate and over a stile into a field and follow the edge of a left-hand wood with views of the Chess valley to your right. At a corner of the wood go straight on across the field, with Sarratt Church soon coming into view ahead, to reach a stile and kissing-gate into the churchyard. Leaving the Chiltern Way and briefly joining **Walk 2**, in the churchyard follow a gravel path passing right of the church.

At a fork in the path keep left, leaving **Walk 2** and going through a lychgate into Church Lane. Turn right onto this road and follow it round a left-hand bend. At a sharp right-hand bend leave the road and take path SA33 straight on over a stile by a gate. Now follow the edge of a wood downhill with a view to your right across the Chess valley to Chorleywood, soon diverging from the edge of the wood and making for a gap in the bottom hedge leading to the remains of a stile. Here bear half right across the next field, climbing to a hedge gap just right of the central of three oaks ahead. Now go straight on across a further field to a hedge gap right of New Model Farm. Here keep straight on through a plantation to join a left-hand hedge at a slight bend in it then follow this hedge downhill to a bridge over the M25. At the far end of the bridge, take a track straight on beside a left-hand hedge for a quarter mile, eventually reaching Solesbridge Lane by New Cottages.

Cross this road and take path SA45, a rough track, straight on, passing through a gap by a padlocked gate by a new house which leads to a concreted farmyard at Micklefield Hall. Go straight on through the farmyard, then, at a crossways by a large oak tree, turn left then almost immediately right into a hedged lane (still path SA45). Follow it straight on for a third of a mile, soon entering a wood called Round Spring where you ignore the three right-hand branching tracks into the wood. On leaving the wood and emerging into a field, follow a right-hand tree-belt straight on to its end. Here bear half left across the field to a stile. Cross this and bear slightly right onto path SA47 following a right-hand hedge to cross a stile by a gate at the far end of the field. Now take path SA46 straight on across the next field to a further stile, then bear half left across another field to a stile left of a flagpole leading into a garden. Here go straight on, keeping left of a hedge to reach a roadside hedge, then follow this hedge, later joining a macadam drive to reach a bend in Sarratt Road. Now take this road straight on to its junction with Little Green Lane on the edge of Croxley Green.

Here turn left onto path SA15, a rough farm road and follow it beside a left-hand hedge for a quarter mile. At a crossways go straight on, then ignore a signposted path to the right and bear slightly left into a hedged lane. On reaching a timber-framed cottage called Oak Farm, take a narrow hedged path straight on. This becomes a fenced path along the edge of a field and ultimately reaches a kissing-gate into Harrocks Wood. Follow an obvious path straight on through this wood ignoring two branching paths to your right. At the far side of the wood go straight on through a squeeze-stile and take a fenced path to a kissing-gate leading to a road junction by the ´Clarendon Arms` at Chandler´s Cross.

Here cross the major road and take Chandler´s Lane straight on uphill for half a mile, recrossing the M25 and passing Potten Farm and Yew Court Farm with its attractive timber buildings and courtyard. At the junction with Templepan Lane, turn left through a kissing-gate onto path SA13 and cross a field diagonally heading for the left-hand end of a copse. On reaching the copse, follow its edge to a macadam farm road, then turn left onto it and follow it to Newhall Farm. Here turn left by a black barn, keeping the barn to your right, then, at the far end of the barn, turn right onto a concrete farm road between a converted barn and a left-hand tractor shed. Follow this concrete road (still path SA13) straight on, leaving the farm and after nearly half a mile reaching a road at Sarratt called Deadman's Ash Hill. Turn left onto this road and follow it for about 100 yards, then, at the end of a right-hand hedge, turn right onto the macadam drive to numbers 1 to 4 The Old Cottages. Where this drive forks, cross a stile in the middle of the fork and take fenced path SA48 straight on to a kissing-gate at the far end of the right-hand garden. Here bear half left across a paddock to cross a stile in its far corner, then follow the left-hand hedge through a second paddock to a kissing-gate at its far end. Now follow the left-hand fence of a tree nursery straight on. Where it bears left, keep straight on across the field to a kissing-gate by the far hedge into a fenced path which leads you out to Sarratt Green near the ´Boot`.

WALK 4:   Flaunden

Length of Walk: (A) 6.5 miles / 10.5 Km
                    (B) 6.0 miles / 9.6 Km
Starting Point: Flaunden village crossroads.
Grid Ref: TL016009
Maps: OS Landranger Sheet 166
          OS Explorer Sheets 172 & 182
          Chiltern Society FP Maps Nos. 5 & 28
How to get there / Parking: Flaunden, 5 miles northwest of
    Rickmansworth, may be reached by leaving the M25 at
    Junction 18 and taking the A404 through Chorleywood
    towards Amersham. After 1.6 miles turn right onto a road
    signposted to Chenies and Latimer and follow its winding
    course for 1.5 miles passing through Chenies and descend-
    ing into the Chess valley. At a crossroads turn right onto the
    Latimer and Flaunden road and follow it straight on for 2
    miles to reach Flaunden. Here ignore a branching road to
    the right and pass the ´Green Dragon`, then either find a
    suitable place to park where the road widens out near a
    telephone box taking care not to obstruct or park opposite
    driveways, or, alternatively, turn left at the crossroads towards
    Bovingdon and find a suitable parking place on that road.
Notes: Both alternative walks are prone to heavy nettle growth in
    summer and deep mud in places even in dry weather.

Flaunden, locally pronounced ´Flarnden` , is an unspoilt secluded
village clustered around a crossroads of narrow lanes on a hilltop
north of the Chess valley. The village church, built in 1838 to
replace a thirteenth-century predecessor over a mile away in the
Chess valley, is notable for being the first to be designed by the
celebrated architect, Sir George Gilbert Scott, who was later
responsible for the Midland Grand Hotel in London which forms
the façade of St. Pancras Station. This church incorporates several
items from its predecessor including its fifteenth-century font, three
ancient bells and the one-handed church clock.

Both walks, which are characterised by a mixture of fine views
and pleasant woodland, lead you down into the idyllically rural
Chess valley at Chenies Bottom, where Walk B follows the valley
bottom, while Walk A climbs the wooded hillside opposite to visit

the picturesque feudal village of Chenies. After Walk A drops again to rejoin Walk B, both routes return to Flaunden by way of the quiet hamlet of Belsize nestling in a Chiltern hollow.

Both walks start from Flaunden village crossroads and take the road signposted to Latimer and Chesham. Go past the ´Green Dragon` then, at a road junction by the church, fork left into a cul-de-sac road (joining the reverse direction of Bucks Walk 8) and follow it for nearly half a mile to a fork by wooden gates. Here fork left into a green lane (leaving Bucks Walk 8 again). After some 25 yards turn right over a stile and take path FD2 beside a left-hand hedge to cross a stile at Martin Top Farm.

Now turn left onto bridleway FD6 between the farm buildings, crossing a concrete road and taking a fenced bridleway straight on across a field. At the far side of the field follow the bridleway turning right to reach a concrete farm road. Now take path FD2a straight on following a right-hand fence, later the outside edge of Baldwin's Wood, gradually descending with views of the Chess valley ahead and Sarratt Church and Goldingtons on a hilltop to your left, to reach a crossing track. Cross this and a stile with wide views of the Chess valley opening out ahead, then, entering Buckinghamshire, take path CN59 straight on downhill, passing just left of an oak tree to reach a stile leading into a farmyard at Mill Farm. Now go straight on through the farmyard to a gate onto the road in Chenies Bottom, where you meet Walk 2A.

Walk B turns left here onto the road joining Walk 2A. Now see the text of Walk 2. **Walk A** bears slightly right onto the road crossing two bridges over arms of the Chess and passing Dodd´s Mill, then, where the road forks, keep right. At a T-junction, cross the major road and take path CN37 into the wood opposite. Just inside the wood, fork left and take a winding path uphill ignoring branching paths to your right to reach a gap by a disused rail-stile. Now take a hedged, later walled path uphill past Chenies Church to the gates of Chenies Manor House.

The church to your left dates from the fifteenth century and is principally notable for the Russell family chapel which was added a century later and houses numerous monuments to the Earls and Dukes of Bedford and other members of the Russell family. The Manor to your right was rebuilt by the first Earl of Bedford in 1530 and was, at one time, known as Chenies Palace, possibly due to both Henry VIII and Elizabeth I staying there several times. The village, whose name derives from the Cheynes family, from whom it passed to the Russells by female succession in 1526, was originally known as Isenhampstead and then Isenhampstead Cheynes. Its name only contracted to its present form in the nineteenth century when a benevolent Duke of Bedford also had many of its cottages rebuilt or improved.

By the Manor gates, turn left down the drive to the picturesque village green. At a crossways, bear slightly left across the green heading for a macadam lane left of a white cottage. Here **Walks 2B and 4A** cross the major road and follow the lane (path CN16) straight on out of the village for nearly half a mile. On reaching Mountwood Farm, just past a white gate to your left, fork right onto a fenced grassy path swinging left. Where the right-hand fence ends, turn immediately left over a stile onto path CN19 and bear slightly right across a field to a stile into Mount Wood. In the wood take a waymarked path straight on downhill, just past the corner of a field forking right over a stile and continuing downhill through a plantation to reach a crossing track. Turn left onto this, crossing a stile by a gate and continuing to Holloway Lane then turn right onto this road to reach a ford and footbridge over the Chess. Cross the bridge, then **Walk 2B** turns right onto a farm road (path SA37) rejoining Walk 2A (now see text of Walk 2); while **Walk 4A** rejoins **Walk 4B** taking path SA36 straight on along the farm road.

At Valley Farm **Walks 4A and 4B** fork right by an oak tree following a right-hand fence to a gate into a hedged path. Take this path straight on, crossing a stile at one point, then ignore a crossing path and bear slightly left through a kissing-gate into the continuation of the hedged path leading to a stile into Hanginglane Wood. Here take the obvious path straight on through the wood to its far side. Now ignore a crossing track and take a stony track straight on through a tree belt. At the far end of the tree belt, leaving the track, follow the left-hand hedge straight on, soon crossing a stile into a field. At the far end of the field cross another stile and bear half left to a hunting-gate leading to fenced path SA25 near Rosehall Farm.

Joining the Chiltern Way, turn sharp right onto this path, soon bearing right and joining a concrete drive, then bearing left and ignoring a branching track to your right. At a further fork bear half right and take a farm road soon passing Rosehall Wood. At the far side of the wood, where the farm road turns left, leave it, forking right over a stile between a gate and an oak tree. Now, leaving the Chiltern Way, head for a house visible through a hedge gap right of a pylon to cross a stile in the next hedge then bear half left to a gate by the corner of a hedge. Here bear half left again to a stile just right of some power-lines. Cross this and turn left onto a road. Just past a cottage, turn right through a hedge gap into Plough Wood, then fork immediately left onto waymarked path SA21 and follow it diagonally across the wood to cross a stile into a field corner. Here follow the outside edge of the wood straight on, then at a corner of the wood,

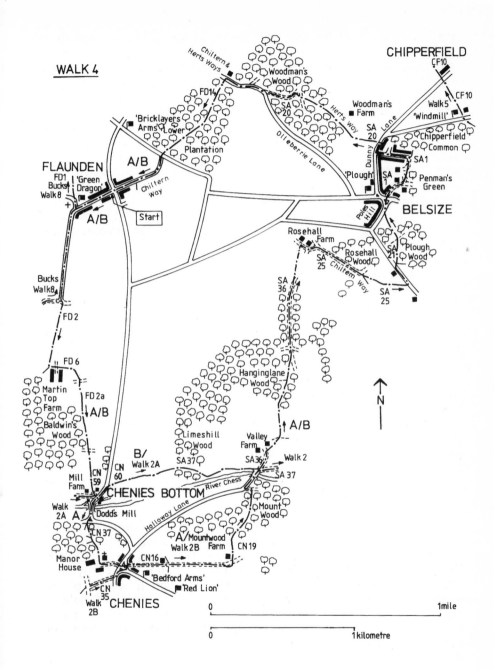

WALK 4

29

bear half right across the field to a stile onto Poles Hill at Belsize.

Cross this road and turn right along its pavement. At a left-hand bend, cross the road again and go straight on across the village green to an entrance left of a telephone box. Here take path SA1, a concreted lane, uphill. Where its concrete surface ends, follow its rough continuation straight on to a fork at the edge of a wood called Penman's Green. Here fork left onto a track into the wood and where it forks, take the lesser right-hand option straight on, soon passing through an anti-horse barrier and joining a gravel drive. Follow this straight on between gateposts, then turn left onto a rough road called Little Windmill Hill which later becomes macadamed and descends to a T-junction.

Here turn right onto the pavement of Dunny Lane and after some 60 yards, joining the Hertfordshire Way, turn left crossing the road and passing through a squeeze-stile by a gate onto path SA20 following a right-hand hedge uphill. At the far end of the field, go straight on into a corner of Woodman's Wood and follow its inside edge straight on. Where woodland commences to your right, take the obvious path straight on for about 200 yards ignoring a crossing bridleway. Now, at a fork, bear left, eventually reaching a gate and gap leading to Olleberrie Lane. Turn right onto this road and follow it for some 350 yards, then just past a cottage called Hollow Hedge, leaving the Hertfordshire Way and rejoining the Chiltern Way, turn left over a stile by a gate onto path FD14 into a wood called Lower Plantation. Take the obvious track straight on along the inside edge of the wood at first, then through the middle of the wood to reach a stile leading to a road junction. Here take the Flaunden and Chenies road straight on for over a quarter mile, leaving the Chiltern Way at the edge of Flaunden and continuing to Flaunden crossroads.

WALK 5:   King's Langley

Length of Walk: 6.8 miles / 11.0 Km
Starting Point: Crossroads near King's Langley cricket pitch.
Grid Ref: TL066028
Maps: OS Landranger Sheet 166
          OS Explorer Sheet 182
          Chiltern Society FP Map No. 5
How to get there / Parking: King's Langley, 2.5 miles southeast
of Hemel Hempstead, may be reached from the town by
taking the A4251 towards Watford. In the village centre, turn
right into Vicarage Lane (signposted to Chipperfield, Sarratt
and Bovingdon) and follow it uphill for 750 yards. Just past
the cricket pitch to your right, turn right at a crossroads into
Love Lane, where there is a parking area on the edge of the
common immediately on your right.

King's Langley, on the western slopes of the Gade valley, now has
its centre along the A4251, near which can be found the fifteenth-
century parish church. This was, however, not always the case, as
the thirteenth-century royal palace and early fourteenth-century
priory were both situated at the top of the hill. Indeed, in mediæval
times the village was for more than two centuries at the centre of the
national stage. King's Langley Palace was built for Queen Eleanor,
wife of Edward I, whose son, later to become Edward II, was
brought up here and as king frequently stayed here. In 1315,
Edward II had his lifelong friend Piers Gaveston buried at the
Priory some two years after the latter had been beheaded by the
Earl of Warwick. Another prominent victim of a violent death to be
buried at the Priory was Richard II, but his remains were later
removed by Henry V for reburial in Westminster Abbey. Prince
Edmund de Langley, the fifth son of Edward III, who was later
made the first Duke of York, was born at the Palace in 1341 and
buried at the Priory in 1402, but, when the latter was suppressed
during the Reformation, his remains were moved to the parish
church, where his tomb can still be seen today. Part of the Palace
was destroyed by fire in the fifteenth century, after which it declined
in importance. Today little remains of this mediæval royal
residence, while of the Priory, only one building has survived which
is now part of the Rudolf Steiner School.

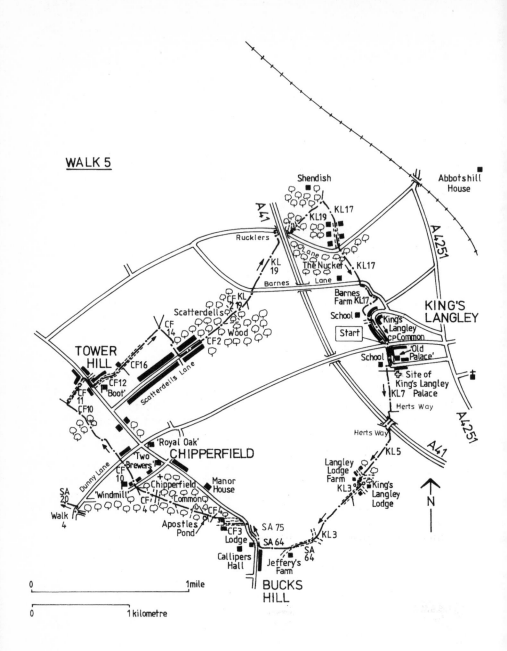

WALK 5

The walk takes you from the attractive common of King's Langley past the sites of the Priory and the Palace across the open, rolling hills southwest of the village to Chipperfield with its wooded common before returning by way of Tower Hill and Shendish to King's Langley.

Starting from the crossroads of Vicarage Lane, Love Lane, Langley Hill and Chipperfield Road, take Langley Hill downhill past the site of the Priory. At a sharp left-hand bend by a pub called the ´Old Palace`, turn right; then, by the entrance to the Rudolf Steiner School, turn left onto path KL7, a narrow alleyway right of a garage, passing between hedges to a kissing-gate. Go through this with a fine view ahead across the Gade valley spanned by the M25 viaduct to Abbot's Langley and the Colne valley beyond, then keep straight on across a field and along a fenced path through a plantation to a kissing-gate on the next rise. Now, briefly joining the Hertfordshire Way, turn right onto path KL8 following a track beside a right-hand fence. Where this track turns right, bear half left to a kissing-gate then continue through scrub to a footbridge over the A41. Cross this bridge, then, leaving the Hertfordshire Way, turn left onto path KL5, descending a bank, then bearing right across a field to a kissing-gate into a plantation. Here fork left, following a left-hand hedge through the plantation to another kissing-gate, then on to a stile into a copse. Go straight on through the copse to a stile leading to a junction of concrete roads by a cottage where an imposing house called King's Langley Lodge can be glimpsed over a gate to your left.

Take the middle option (path KL3) straight on past a Georgian house, then bearing left past a large pond. By a modern house and farm buildings, turn right, keeping the farm buildings to your left and the house to your right, to leave the farm by way of a stile by a gate. Now follow a left-hand fence straight on through two fields, ignoring the stile of a branching path to your left and later descending to cross a stile in a thick hedge. Now bear half left uphill across a field to a gate and squeeze-stile at the left-hand end of a clump of trees. Go through the squeeze-stile and turn right onto a sunken track (bridleway SA64). Follow this uphill for about 300 yards, then, after it levels off, at a left-hand bend just short of Jeffrey's Farm, the reputed home of President Jimmy Carter's ancestors, leave the track and take path SA64, heading half right across a field towards a tall redwood tree on the skyline, joining a left-hand fence to reach the corner of a garden hedge. Here bear half right again to a stile leading to hedged bridleway SA75. Turn right onto this and follow it beside a road called Bucks Hill until it joins the road opposite the corner of Chipperfield's wooded common.

Here cross the road and take path CF3 along the gated macadam access road opposite to the end of this road at the gates to Little Callipers. Here turn right onto path CF4, entering woodland right of a yew tree and continuing through hollybushes. At a T-junction of paths, turn left, soon passing an overgrown pond to your left and going straight on to reach the Apostles´ Pond. This pond is so named because it used to be surrounded by twelve ancient lime trees which had to be replaced by young trees in 1984 which will take some years to mature. Go straight on past this pond, then, at a fork, take the left-hand option. Follow this path straight on through the woods for nearly half a mile, ignoring all crossing paths, until houses come into sight ahead. Here at a fork, take the left-hand option to reach a road at Chipperfield by a signpost just right of the ´Windmill` pub which stands on or near the site of a windmill shown on the 1822 Ordnance Survey map. The village church built in 1837 and the other village pubs can be reached by taking the road to your right.

Cross this road and take the narrow, fenced path CF10 between gardens to a kissing-gate into a field. Now go straight on downhill to a gate and kissing-gate in front of the last house in a row in Dunny Lane. Bear slightly left across this road and go through a kissing-gate frame beside a gate, then follow a right-hand hedge uphill through a field to a hedge gap. Go through this and continue to follow the right-hand hedge, turning left then right. On entering a copse, go straight on through it to a stile at its far side, then follow a right-hand hedge to cross a stile at the far end of the field. Now bear right through a thicket into a wide hedged lane (bridleway CF11), which leads you to a road at the hamlet of Tower Hill.

Turn right along this road and ignore New Road to your left. Just before the ´Boot`, turn left into a lane (path CF12, later CF16) and follow it for a third of a mile until you enter a field. Now follow a right-hand hedge straight on. After a quarter mile, where the hedge turns right, follow it joining path CF14. At a corner of the field, go through a kissing-gate and follow a fenced path along the edge of Scatterdells Wood, wiggling to the right and soon reaching Scatterdells Lane. Turn left onto this residential road and follow it to its end. Here go straight on over a stile by a gate onto path CF2 into Scatterdells Wöod. At a fork just inside the wood, bear right, following a flinty track beside a left-hand fence. Where the fence bears away to the left, at a three-way fork, take the central option, following a waymarked track straight on, ignoring a crossing path in a dip, a crossing track beyond it and a track branching to the right. Now cross a stile and take path KL19, bearing half left across a field to a kissing-gate into Barnes Lane.

Cross this road and go through a kissing-gate opposite, then bear half right, heading towards Shendish House hidden in trees on the next hilltop. On reaching a clump of trees right of the A41 bridge over Rucklers Lane, bear slightly left and follow a right-hand hedge, then a fence downhill to a kissing-gate into Rucklers Lane. Turn right onto this road passing under the A41. After about 120 yards, turn left onto the right-hand of two drives (still path KL19) and follow this uphill through a wood. Where the drive forks, take a narrow path straight on to cross a stile into Shendish Park. Now go straight on through a plantation to reach a belt of large trees concealing Shendish House, then turn right and follow the edge of the tree belt, gradually bearing left to reach a corner near a wooden junction signpost.

Here turn sharp right onto path KL17, doubling back across the plantation, with a fine view to your left across the Gade valley including Abbotshill House, now a school, on the other side of the valley, and heading for a gate and stile right of a brick and flint cottage. Cross this stile and take a wide hedged track straight on downhill to cross Rucklers Lane at the bottom. Now go through a kissing-gate and climb a series of flights of steps straight on through a wood called The Nucket to a kissing-gate, then follow a right-hand hedge straight on across a field to a kissing-gate leading to Barnes Lane. Cross this road, then go through a hedge gap with a redundant ladder stile opposite and turn immediately left onto a path (still KL17) between the roadside hedge and a school playing field fence. After about 250 yards, turn right, leaving the roadside hedge and continuing to follow the playing field fence for some 350 yards until you emerge at the school entrance. Here turn left onto the school drive, then immediately right into Love Lane and follow it back to your starting point.

WALK 6: Hemel Hempstead Station

Length of Walk: 5.9 miles / 9.5 Km
Starting Point: Forecourt of Hemel Hempstead Station.
Grid Ref: TL043059
Maps: OS Landranger Sheet 166
OS Explorer Sheet 182
Chiltern Society FP Maps Nos. 5 & 20
Parking: Hemel Hempstead Station is located just off the A4251 at Boxmoor about 1 mile southwest of the town centre. At the mini-roundabout by the station, turn off the main road into Fishery Road, crossing Boxmoor Common and the canal bridge by the 'Fishery Inn`, then seek an on-street parking space in one of the side streets.

Since the war, Hemel Hempstead, at the confluence of the rivers Gade and Bulbourne, has developed into a large modern town due to its designation in the late 1940s as a 'new town`. Despite this, the surrounding countryside has retained its rural atmosphere and even the town itself is less of a concrete jungle than some of its counterparts, thanks to the preservation of 'green lungs` particularly along the river valleys. Hemel Hempstead also has a long history as its southern part is traversed by a Roman road known as Akeman Street and remains of Roman villas have been found not only here but also in Gadebridge Park to the north of the town centre. In the Middle Ages, Hemel Hempstead must already have been a wealthy market town as is attested by its magnificent twelfth-century church and in the eighteenth and nineteenth centuries, the construction of the Grand Junction Canal, the L&NWR main line to the Midlands and North and several paper mills where modern paper-making methods were pioneered, all to the south of the mediæval town, caused its expansion southwards.

The walk soon leaves the town behind, climbing the wooded southern slope of the Bulbourne valley to Felden and the rural upland plateau beyond to reach Bovingdon Church. The return route then takes you by way of Stoney Lane and the Westbrook Hay golf course with its fine views of the Bulbourne valley, to Bourne End and the Grand Union Canal at Winkwell Swing Bridge, probably the most picturesque location on the Chilterns section of the canal, before following its towpath back to the station.

36

Starting from the main entrance to Hemel Hempstead Station, turn left out of the station past a small car park to cross the A4251 just left of a mini-roundabout. Now turn left along its pavement and follow it under a railway bridge and the A41 bridge, then cross the A4251 again and joining the Chiltern Way, take fenced path HH136 bearing left along the foot of the A41 embankment. By a pedestrian tunnel bear half right passing between bollards and through a kissing-gate frame, then take hedged path HH99 uphill to a kissing-gate. Go through this, then fork right onto path HH100 climbing through woodland and soon joining a drive. Some 15 yards beyond a right-hand bend fork left onto a path through the woods. On reaching a flinty track (byway HH101), turn right onto it, soon reaching Felden Lane, then turn left onto this road and follow it uphill into Felden.

Where the road bears left by the entrance to Roefields Close, fork half right onto path HH105, a macadam drive leading to Felden Lodge, and follow this through a wood and out onto a golf course. Halfway across the golf course by two ash trees to your right, leave the drive and bear half left to reach a kissing-gate. Go through this and a second kissing-gate then bear half right across a field to pass through a third kissing-gate by a garage right of a house and bungalow. Here cross a drive and follow a left-hand hedge to cross a stile into a field, then follow a right-hand hedge straight on to a squeeze-stile leading to Longcroft Lane.

Turn right onto this road and follow it past a large house called Felden Barns to a sharp left-hand bend. Here leave the road and take path HH112 straight on over a stile and across a field to a hedge gap at the far side of the field. Now on path BV16, bear half right across a second field to join the edge of Bury Wood by a clump of trees in the field concealing a pond. Bear slightly left here and follow the outside edge of the wood, later a right-hand hedge, straight on to the far end of the field. Here go through a metal hunting-gate and follow a fenced path along the edge of a right-hand copse to another hunting-gate. Now turn right and follow the right-hand hedge around a field corner and then straight on along the edge of a prairie field for over half a mile to pass through a kissing-gate at the far end of the field. Here, leaving the Chiltern Way, take path BV17 bearing half right across a field towards Bovingdon Church to a hunting-gate, then continue straight on to a kissing-gate, then along a hedged path to a V-stile leading to Church Street, Bovingdon opposite the church.

Set in one of the largest churchyards in Hertfordshire, Bovingdon Church was rebuilt in 1845 on the site of a thirteenth-century predecessor, from which the effigy of a knight dating from around 1400 is preserved. The village to your left has some attractive old cottages, but has been rather swamped by modern development.

37

Fork right onto the road passing the church, then at a sharp left-hand bend, joining the Hertfordshire Way, turn right onto byway BV20 (Stoney Lane), a macadam road soon becoming a rough lane, following it straight on for half a mile until you reach a number of houses. By a right-hand house with lattice windows called Huntsmoor, turn left onto a macadam residential road called Bushfield Road and follow it out to the B4505.

Turn right onto this road, passing a brick-and-flint lodge to your left. Just past this lodge, cross the road and take a macadam drive opposite (path BV23), ignoring a bridlegate to your right and almost immediately turning right over a stile by a gate. Now keep left at a fork and take an obvious path straight on through Gorsefield Wood, eventually emerging onto a macadam golf club road. Turn right onto this road following it past the car park and the clubhouse, then bearing left to some former farm buildings. Just past these buildings, the road turns right and where it ends, keep left of a hedge and follow it straight on, then continue along a grassy track (still path BV23) with fine views ahead across the Bulbourne valley with Berkhamsted to your left and the edge of Hemel Hempstead to your right.

Having passed two bungalows, go straight on past a rustic seat, then, by a junction signpost and a protruding oak tree, turn left, passing just right of a clump of trees with the fifth green to your right. Also to your right is an imposing early nineteenth-century manor house called Westbrook Hay, at one time the offices of the Hemel Hempstead New Town Development Corporation. Now keep straight on downhill passing right of the fourth green then bearing slightly left and taking bridleway BV32 over a bridge across the A41. At the far end of the bridge, take the fenced bridleway wending its way downhill to a gate and stile, then continue straight on along fenced byway HH115 into a green lane leading to the A4251 at Bourne End.

Cross this road and turn right onto its footway. After 350 yards, just before a petrol station, turn left down a narrow lane called Winkwell, soon crossing a narrow bridge over the River Bulbourne. On reaching the Winkwell Swing Bridge over the Grand Union Canal, opposite the picturesque sixteenth-century 'Three Horseshoes', turn right onto the canal towpath. Now follow the towpath in its deceptively rural setting frequented by ducks and fishermen, for just over a mile, passing under a railway bridge and later a small road bridge. On reaching a second road bridge by the 'Fishery Inn', climb a shallow flight of steps to Fishery Road, then turn right and almost immediately left, crossing the road and passing through a kissing-gate. Now take macadam path HH98 across Boxmoor Common to another kissing-gate and a pelican crossing on the A4251 where the railway station is in front of you.

WALK 6

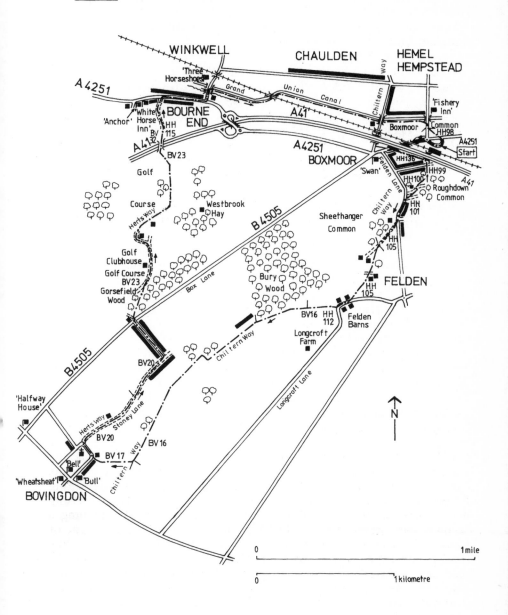

WALK 7:   Berkhamsted (North)

Length of Walk: (A) 7.9 miles / 12.7 Km
                    (B) 2.1 miles / 3.4 Km
                    (C) 5.2 miles / 8.3 Km
Starting Point: (A/B) Mini-roundabout by northern entrance
                         to Berkhamsted railway station.
                  (C) Potten End village hall.
Grid Ref: (A/B) SP994082
                (C) TL016089
Maps: OS Landranger Sheets 165 (A/B only) & 166 (all)
        OS Explorer Sheets 181 (A/B only) & 182 (A/C only)
        Chiltern Society FP Map No.20
How to get there / Parking: (A/B) From the junction of the old
      A4251 and A416 in Berkhamsted town centre, take the
      Potten End road and park either in the car park on the left or
      at the railway station.
      (C) Potten End. 1.8 miles northeast of Berkhamsted, may be
      reached from the town by taking one of several signposted
      routes. On reaching the village green, ignore two turnings to
      the right and park in a small car park on your right opposite
      the village hall.
Notes: Heavy nettle growth may be encountered in summer
      particularly on path GG68 on Walks A and C.

Berkhamsted, with its centre in the bottom of a steep-sided river valley, is, in many ways, a typical Chiltern town as it has spread first along its valley and later up the hills on either side. Nevertheless its history sets it apart from its neighbours. In 1066, William the Conqueror, following his victory at the Battle of Hastings, passed through the town on his circuitous approach to London and here accepted the surrender of the Saxon nobles. Shortly after this, he gave the manor to his half-brother, Robert of Mortain who built a castle in this strategically important defile through the Chilterns as a way of protecting London from possible attack. This castle was later destroyed and was rebuilt by the famous Archbishop of Canterbury, Thomas à Becket. The ruins of this castle, which was last occupied in 1496, can still be seen today near the railway station. Amongst the prominent names linked with the castle are the Black Prince, who lived in it as Duke of Cornwall,

King John of France who was imprisoned here in 1361 and the poet, Geoffrey Chaucer, who was at one time its clerk of works. Another poet associated with the town is William Cowper, born the son of its rector in 1731, and monuments both to him and his mother are to be found in the thirteenth-century parish church, one of the largest in Hertfordshire.

Walks A and B lead you from the town to its extensive heathy and wooded common returning with fine views over the town, while Walks A and C explore the quiet ridges and valleys beyond with their small picturesque villages and scenic views.

Starting from the mini-roundabout by the northern entrance to Berkhamsted railway station, **Walks A and B** take Brownlow Road northwards past the ruins of Berkhamsted Castle. At a right-hand bend, fork left onto Castle Hill and follow this road straight on uphill. At a left-hand bend by the entrance to Berkhamsted Cricket, Sports and Social Club, leave the road and take path BK1 straight on over a stile into a private car park, then follow a private road straight on to a second car park. Now take a grassy track straight on beside a powerline to a gate and stile, then follow a left-hand fence straight on through three fields to a gate and stile leading to a track junction at Well Farm. Here turn right onto the right-hand track (path NC58), passing right of the farm buildings, then climbing to join a macadam drive by a bungalow. Where this drive bears right, leave it and take bridleway NC56 straight on into scrubby woodland.

After 50 yards at a crossways, **Walk B** turns right onto bridleway NC57, soon reaching New Road. Cross this, bearing slightly right and continue uphill (still on bridleway NC57). At a fork bear left and on emerging onto a golf course, go straight on to the left-hand side of a clump of bushes, then bear right through the bushes to reach a rough road. Turn right onto this road rejoining **Walk A** then read the last paragraph.

At the crossways, **Walk A** takes bridleway NC56 straight on. On reaching a track near New Road to your right, take a permissive bridleway straight on to a gravel car park. Now bear right to a road junction near a war memorial. Here cross the major road and take bridleway NP23 straight on, passing right of the war memorial, crossing a golf fairway and keeping left at a fork. In the next tree belt, look out for a signposted fork to the left. Fork left onto this defined path and follow it straight on across a fairway and through a tree belt, then bear half right across another fairway to enter concealed, waymarked path NP18 between gardens right of a clump broom bushes.

Walks A and C follow this path to cross a residential road called

Frithsden Copse, then take a fenced path straight on. On entering Great Frithsden Copse, disregard a crossing path and go straight on for some 400 yards. Where another path merges from your right, bear slightly left and continue downhill to a road at the scattered hamlet of Frithsden (pronounced 'Freezeden').

Turn right onto this road passing two houses, then, after about 80 yards, turn left through a gap in a wall under a tree onto fenced path NP19 and follow it to a stile. Cross this and follow a right-hand hedge uphill. On reaching an earth bund near Highridge Farm, cross a stile a few yards to your right and follow a fenced path past the farm to a stile leading to a stony track on the ridgetop, where Ashridge House, rebuilt for the seventh Earl of Bridgewater by Wyatt in the early nineteenth century, comes into view on a hill to your left. Turn right onto this track and follow it through two fields. On reaching double gates, turn left to cross a further stile leading to a rough road known locally as 'Roman Road'.

Now ignore a kissing-gate to your left and turn left onto the rough road. Where it starts to descend into a walled cutting constructed for the canal-building third Duke of Bridgewater, fork right through a squeeze-stile by a gate onto path NP8 turning left over a stile into a belt of trees. Now follow this path downhill through the tree belt beside the sunken way, passing an old bridge over the sunken way and continuing downhill to reach a flight of steps descending to rejoin the road. Now follow this downhill into Nettleden, a tiny village with picturesque seventeenth-century cottages and a church rebuilt in brick in 1811 but retaining its fifteenth-century tower.

At a T-junction, turn left onto a road passing double gates, then turn right through an anti-horse barrier onto path NP9, following a right-hand hedge uphill through three fields with a left-hand hedge enclosing the path in places and an enclosing left-hand fence in the second and third fields. Now cross a stile and take enclosed path GG76, eventually joining a gravel drive which leads to a road at St. Margaret's, named after the former twelfth-century nunnery of St. Margaret de Bosco.

Turn left onto this road, then, after about 50 yards, (re)joining the Hertfordshire Way, turn right over a concealed stile by a gate onto path GG78. Now bear slightly left, following the outside edge of St. Margaret´s Copse downhill to a stile. Here leave the wood and go straight on across a field, passing right of a clump of hawthorn bushes, then bearing slightly left to cross a stile by a gate leading to a hedge gap by a twin-poled electricity pylon. Go through this gap and take path GG1, bearing half right across a field to a stile and kissing-gate in the far corner of the field on the edge of Great Gaddesden. Leaving the Hertfordshire Way, go through the kissing-gate and take path GG2 following the churchyard wall beneath a row of lime trees. At the far end of the churchyard, turn left over a stile into it and follow a right-hand wall through the churchyard to a lychgate.

Great Gaddesden's twelfth-century church with its massive fifteenth-century tower decorated with gargoyles is notable for the Roman bricks used in its construction, which are believed to have derived from a Roman villa on the same site, and the early Georgian Halsey mausoleum containing more than twenty monuments.

Now go through the lychgate and take a road, bearing right and ignoring a turning to the left. At a T-junction turn right, then immediately left onto fenced path GG68 leading to a stile into a field. Now follow a left-hand hedge straight on to a kissing-gate at the far side of the field. Do **not** use this kissing-gate, but pass through a gap to its right and turn right onto fenced path GG67, following it uphill into Highpark Wood. Just inside the wood, turn left onto path GG69 and follow it along the inside edge of the wood for nearly half a mile with views to your left at first across Water End in the Gade valley towards Gaddesden Place on the hill opposite, built by Wyatt for the Halseys in 1768-1773 and still their home today. On reaching a T-junction ofpaths, turn left rejoining path GG67, soon crossing a stile into a field with a view across the valley towards Potten End on the next ridge. Now go straight on downhill heading for the corner of a hedge on the hillside opposite to reach a stile onto Nettleden Road.

Cross this road and go through a kissing-gate opposite, then follow a right-hand fence straight on, ignoring a branching path to your left and (now on path NP31) continuing to a field corner. Here turn left and follow a right-hand fence to the corner of a hedge, then turn right and take a fenced path beside a left-hand hedge to a kissing-gate into a wood. Now follow the fenced path straight on along the edge of the wood to another kissing-gate where you turn left and follow a left-hand fence uphill ignoring a branching path to your right. Soon the path becomes enclosed between garden fences and you continue uphill passing through another kissing-gate and eventually reaching Water End Road on the edge of Potten End. Turn right onto its pavement and follow the major road straight on for half a mile, ignoring all side turnings, to reach the village hall.

From Potten End village hall, where **Walk C** starts, **Walks A and C** follow the Berkhamsted road to the edge of the village green, then opposite Bullbeggars Lane, signposted to Bourne End, (re)joining the Hertfordshire Way, turn right onto bridleway NP22, the left-hand of two tracks into woodland, ignoring all lesser branching paths to your right and left and later following back garden fences to your right. On reaching a sunken gully, part of the ancient earthwork known as Grim's Ditch, enter it and follow it straight on for a quarter mile, crossing a golf course at one point, to reach Nettleden Road. Turn right onto this road, then almost immediately left.

Now **Walk C** takes the right-hand of two bridleways (NP24) straight on, ignoring all lesser branching paths. On emerging onto the golf course, bear slightly left, following an obvious path passing left of the 16th tee and right of the 15th green and heading towards a prominent birch tree on the edge of the wood ahead. Just before reaching this tree, leaving the Hertfordshire Way, turn right onto waymarked path NP18 between gardens. Now go back to the top of page 44.

Walk A leaves the Hertfordshire Way and takes the left-hand of the two bridleways (NP23) and follows its winding course through woodland, ignoring lesser branching paths and soon reaching a fairway. Go straight on across this into further woodland. Here keep right at a fork, then go straight on, crossing two further fairways to pass left of the war memorial and reach a road junction. Now turn left onto the Potten End and Water End road and follow it to the entrance to Berkhamsted Golf Club, then turn right onto it. Where the macadam road ends, take a gravel road straight on.

At the end of the road by the gate of Fairhill, **Walks A and B** bear half right onto path BK2 into woodland, keeping left at a fork and following a garden wall to a kissing-gate. Here continue over a stile with a superb view across Berkhamsted beginning to open out ahead, then follow a left-hand fence, passing left of two cattle grids. Now follow the left-hand hedge generally straight on through three fields. At the far end of the third field, turn right and follow a left-hand hedge, later a line of beech trees downhill to a kissing-gate onto New Road opposite the ruins of Berkhamsted Castle. Cross the road, then turn left onto its pavement and follow it to a crossroads. Here fork right into a road called White Hill and follow it beside the railway back to Berkhamsted Station.

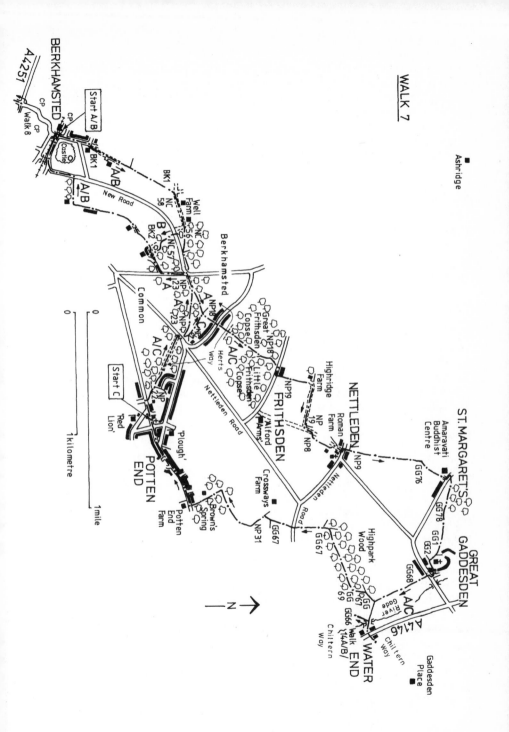

WALK 7

45

WALK 8:   Berkhamsted (South)

Length of Walk: 8.3 miles / 13.3 Km
Starting Point: Junction of A4251 (High Street) and A416
         (Kings Road), Berkhamsted.
Grid Ref: SP991079
Maps: OS Landranger Sheet 165
      OS Explorer Sheet 181 (or old Sheet 2)
      Chiltern Society FP Maps Nos. 8 & 17
Parking: There are several public car parks in the centre of
Berkhamsted.
Notes: Heavy nettle growth may be found in summer on
bridleway AG2 and path BK46.

Berkhamsted, the name of which is locally pronounced 'Berk´msted` and has, till quite recently, been prone to a number of variations in spelling, is described in the introduction to Walk 7.

The walk takes you westwards uphill through leafy suburbs to cross the bypass and continue by way of the lost village of Marlin to the hilltop Buckinghamshire village of Hawridge with its moated manor house. From here, it takes you south-eastwards along the crest of a ridge and then down into Chesham Vale before returning by way of Ashley Green and Hockeridge Wood to Berkhamsted.

Starting from the junction of the A4251 (High Street) and the A416 (Kings Road), take Kings Road uphill. After some 200 yards, turn right into Charles Street, then take the second turning left, Doctors´ Commons Road. Opposite No.19, turn right into a fenced alleyway (path BK14). Follow this straight on, joining a right-hand road for a few yards and then leaving it again, crossing a drive and eventually emerging into North Road. Turn left into this road, then immediately right into Anglefield Road and after about 25 yards, fork left onto path BK15, an alleyway left of a double garage and follow it straight on to reach Cross Oak Road, a narrow lane without pavements. Turn left into this lane and ignore first a left-hand turn, then a right-hand turn called Greystoke Close. Opposite a house called Chilterns, turn right onto path BK18, a fenced alleyway by the entrance to Little Corner and follow it straight on, crossing another alley and two roads and eventually emerging onto Shootersway at the edge of the town.

Turn right onto this road, then immediately left through a gap by gates into a rough lane (bridleway BK33) and follow it downhill. At the bottom, on entering a field, take path NC21a, following a left-hand hedge straight on uphill to a stile in the bypass fence. Cross this stile and turn right to descend a flight of steps then cross the A41 via a gap in its central reservation crash-barrier and climb another flight of steps to a stile. Here join bridleway NC21 following a rough track straight on beside a left-hand hedge. Where the track passes through a hedge gap into another field, continue to follow it straight on, now with a hedge to your right. Near the far end of this field, follow the track reverting to the other side of the hedge. Now take bridleway NC20, a wide grassy lane, straight on, keeping left of a wood called Cock Grove and passing Marlin Chapel Farm, where there are traces of a moat and it would appear that there might once have been a village.

Where the lane opens out into a plantation, leave the track, bearing slightly right and passing right of the ruins of St. Mary Magdalene's Chapel (already a ruin in 1822) to a gate and stile into Rossway Park with a view of Rossway House ahead. Now go straight on across the park, gradually diverging from a left-hand fence to reach a stile left of a bungalow on the far side of the park. Cross this stile and a rough lane and take path WG4 straight on through a hedge gap, following a right-hand hedge downhill to a stile in the valley bottom. Cross this and turn right onto a road following the Buckinghamshire boundary; then at a fork, bear left onto the road signposted to Wigginton and Tring. Just past a right-hand copse, turn left through a gap in the roadside bank onto bridleway CY36, following the left-hand side of a strip of grass, later a hedge uphill to reach a metal gate. Do **not** go through this gate, but instead turn left onto path CY38 and follow a right-hand hedge, soon passing a plantation to reach a stile. Cross this stile, then turn left and follow a left-hand hedge to a field corner. Here turn right and continue to follow the left-hand hedge through two fields to a stile into a rough lane near Hill Farm.

Turn right into the lane and follow it downhill, bearing right at the bottom to reach a road junction by Vale Farm on the edge of Hawridge Common. Turn sharp left onto the road, then immediately fork right opposite a rusty white gate onto path CY48, climbing across the wooded common to emerge onto a road at the top of the hill opposite Church Lane. Cross this road and take Church Lane straight on to reach Hawridge Church with its green-painted bellcote, built in 1856 on the site of its thirteenth-century predecessor, and Hawridge Court, a timber-framed manor house with a partially filled moat.

By the entrance to Hawridge Court, turn right onto path CY56, a narrow alleyway between a hedge and a cottage, to reach a stile into a field where the moat is visible to your left. In the field, turn left onto path CY31, briefly joining Bucks Walk 6. Now cross a stile by a gate in the corner of the field and follow a left-hand hedge through the next field to a stile at the far side. Cross this and follow the crest of the ridge straight on through two large fields with fine views of Hawridge Vale to your left, a Victorian house called Thorne Barton on a hilltop near Ashley Green ahead and the outskirts of Chesham further to the right. After nearly three-quarters of a mile, at the far end of the second field, go through a hedge gap then turn left and follow the left-hand hedge downhill to a corner of the field. Here turn right and continue to follow a left-hand hedge to the bottom corner of the field. Now turn left over a stile onto path CY54, a grassy hedged lane, and follow it straight on. At the far end of the lane bear slightly right over a stile and take a fenced path to reach a gate and stile leading to the road in Chesham Vale.

Turn left onto this road joining Bucks Walk 7. Opposite the 'Black Horse', turn right onto bridleway CY51 (later AG1c), a rough sunken lane, and follow it straight on for a quarter mile. Where the lane forks and the left-hand option goes straight on to a gate into a wood, turn right onto bridleway AG2; then, where the main track turns right again through large green gates, leave it and take a narrower sunken track straight on, climbing gradually through a copse and past a pond. At the top of the hill, follow the lane bearing left and continuing between hedges for some 300 yards until you reach the end of a concrete farm road. Go straight on along this, crossing a stile by a gate to reach Flamstead Farm. Here turn left (still on bridleway AG2) and leaving Bucks Walk 7, pass left of a Dutch barn to a gate into another hedged lane, which you follow for a quarter mile to reach a road called Hog Lane on the edge of Ashley Green.

Cross this road and take fenced path AG2e straight on to a kissing-gate into a field, then follow a left-hand hedge straight on to the corner of the field. Here transfer through a gap in the left-hand hedge to its other side and follow it downhill turning left then right at one point, to reach a kissing-gate into Hockeridge Wood. Now ignore a crossing path and take a woodland track straight on for a third of a mile, disregarding various branching or crossing tracks. On passing a small picnic area to your right, by a white noticeboard, turn right onto path AG17a, a grassy track and follow this downhill, keeping left at a fork, to reach a crossing track at the bottom marking the county boundary. Cross this and take path BK46 straight on uphill. Near a right-hand bungalow, where the path turns left, leave it bearing right to cross a stile out of the wood. Now follow the outside edge of the wood straight on to a corner of the wood, then bear half right across the field to gates and a kissing-gate under an oak tree leading to the A416.

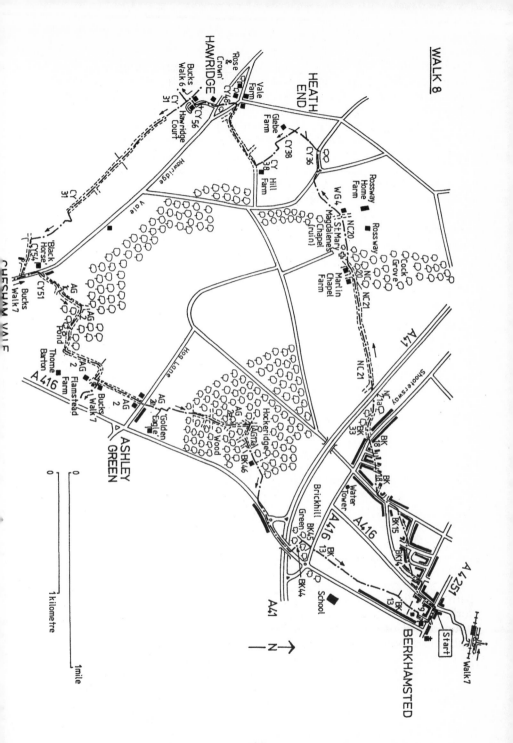

WALK 8

49

Turn left onto this road and follow it to a new roundabout. Here take the A416 straight on to cross a bridge over the bypass. At the far end of the bridge, turn left over a stile onto path BK44 and follow it through woodland known as Brickhill Green. At the far side of the wood, turn right onto path BK45 and follow it along the inside edge of the wood to the A416. Cross this main road bearing slightly left and take path BK13 up steps and through a kissing-gate. Now follow a line of trees straight on across a school playing field with views across Berkhamsted to the hills beyond. At the far side, take an alleyway straight on downhill, soon passing a field to your right, to reach another school playing field. Go straight on along the edge of tbis playing field then take an alleyway left of a school (path BK9) straight on, soon turning right to reach the end of a cul-de-sac called Prince Edward Street. Turn left to reach the High Street, then left again for your starting point.

WALK 9:   Northchurch Common

Length of Walk: 6.9 miles / 11.2 Km
Starting Point: Informal car park at bend in B4506 half a mile
north of Northchurch.
Grid Ref: SP979095
Maps: OS Landranger Sheet 165
OS Explorer Sheet 181 (or old Sheet 2)
Chiltern Society FP Maps Nos. 17 & 19
How to get there / Parking: Northchurch Common, 1.5 miles
northwest of Berkhamsted, may be reached from the town by
taking the A4251 northwestwards to Northchurch, then
turning right onto the B4506 and following it for half a mile
to a sharp left-hand bend. Here ignore a turning to the right,
then almost immediately turn right into a grassy car park.

Northchurch Common on the hill above Northchurch is one of a
belt of largely wooded commons stretching from the outskirts of
Berkhamsted to Aldbury and Ivinghoe Beacon now managed by
the National Trust. The village in the Bulbourne valley below,
which you skirt early in the walk, is today little more than a suburb
of nearby Berkhamsted, but it was once more important than its
urban neighbour. In Roman times, Northchurch was the site of a
small town and in Saxon times it had a castle and a stone-built
church, part of which is incorporated in the present largely
thirteenth-century building. In the church is a brass memorial to
Peter the Wildboy who became famous in 1725 after being found
living wild in the woods near Hamelin in King George I´s country
of birth and joint kingdom, the Electorate of Hanover. Peter was
brought to England by the King, but, when it proved impossible to
educate him, he was sent to a farm in Northchurch where he spent
the rest of his left and was buried in 1785. In more modern times,
although the relative importance of Northchurch has declined, its
location on various major transport routes through the Chilterns
has caused it to grow and develop into a commuter dormitory.

    The walks first leads you down towards Northchurch to join the
Grand Union Canal towpath and follow it for over a mile to Cow
Roast Lock. Having left the canal, you walk over a hill to the
picturesque village of Aldbury before climbing the wooded
escarpment to reach the Bridgewater Monument. From here, the

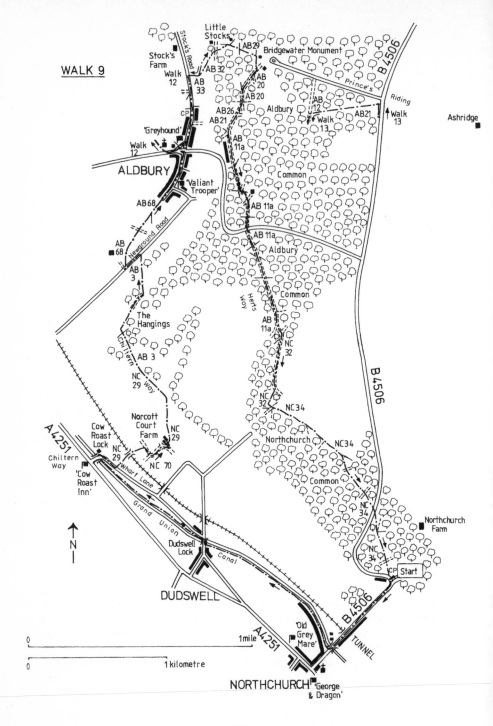

WALK 9

Little Stocks
AB29
Stock's Road
Bridgewater Monument
Stock's Farm
Walk 12
AB 32
AB 20
AB 33
AB 20
Prince's
Riding
B 4506
AB26
Aldbury
AB 12
Walk 13
Ashridge
CP
AB21
Walk 13
AB21
Walk 13
'Greyhound'
Walk 12
AB 11a
ALDBURY
Common
'Valiant Trooper'
AB68
AB 11a
Newground Road
AB 11a
AB 68
Aldbury
AB 3
Common
Herts Way
The Hangings
Chiltern Way
AB 3
AB 11a
NC 32
NC 29
NC 32
NC 32
NC34
A 4251
Cow Roast Lock
Norcott Court Farm
NC 29
Northchurch
NC34
NC34
Chiltern Way
NC 29
Wharf Lane
NC 70
Northchurch Farm
'Cow Roast Inn'
Grand Union
Common
NC 34
N
Dudswell Lock
Canal
NC 34
CP Start
DUDSWELL
B 4506
'Old Grey Mare'
A 4251
TUNNEL
B 4506
0   1mile
0   1 kilometre
NORTHCHURCH 'George & Dragon'

52

walk returns by way of Aldbury's wooded common and Northchurch Common with its mixture of open grassland and heathland to your starting point.

Starting from the entrance to the car park, turn left onto the B4506 and follow it downhill towards Northchurch for nearly half a mile to the bridge over the Grand Union Canal on the edge of the village. Having crossed this bridge, turn right through a gap by a gate onto the canal towpath at Northchurch Lock. Follow this pleasant waterside path northwestwards for three-quarters of a mile to a road bridge at Dudswell. Turn right over this bridge, then immediately left rejoining the towpath at Dudswell Lock and following it for over half a mile to bridge no.137 at Cow Roast Lock, the name of which is thought to be a corruption of 'Cow Rest' as the nearby 'Cow Roast Inn' may have been a resting place for cattle drovers on their way down the modern A4251 to the London markets.

Pass under the bridge, climb a flight of steps to the lock, then turn sharp right between walls to reach Wharf Lane. Joining the Chiltern Way, turn left onto this road and follow it for about 150 yards, then turn left over a stile onto path NC29 and go straight across a field to an ungainly footbridge over the railway. Having crossed this bridge, keep straight on across the next field to a hedge gap. Go through this gap then turn right onto fenced bridleway NC70, soon turning left onto the fenced continuation of path NC29 and passing through a gap by a gate at Norcott Court Farm.

Here bear half right up a drive. At a junction of drives, turn left then cross a stile by a gate and turn right, keeping right of farm buildings to cross a stile by a gate. Now bear half left, crossing the field diagonally with fine views across the Bulbourne valley to your left and behind you, to cross a stile by a gate in the far corner. Here follow a right-hand deer-fence across the next field to the corner of a hedge, then follow this hedge straight on to a corner of the field. Now turn right through a hedge gap and belt of trees, then climb steps to a stile. Here take path AB3 bearing half left across a field to a stile in the top left-hand corner where a fine view opens out through the Tring Gap towards the Aylesbury Vale beyond. Cross this stile and follow the edge of a right-hand wood called The Hangings straight on, ignoring a crossing byway (where you leave the Chiltern Way). At the corner of the wood turn right, following the edge of the wood for a further 200 yards, with a fine view ahead of Aldbury hidden in trees backed by Clipper Down, then cross a stile by a gate into a hedged lane and follow it along the edge of the wood. At the far end of this lane, bear half left across two fields, with the top of the Bridgewater Monument visible over the treetops to your right, to cross a stile by the end of a belt of trees. Now turn left to reach a stile onto Newground Road.

Turn left onto this road, then at a left-hand bend, just before a concrete drive, turn right through a gate onto path AB68 and cross a field diagonally to pass through a handgate. Now turn right, following a right-hand hedge to cross a stile at the far end of the field, then follow a left-hand hedge straight on to cross a further stile into a hedged path. Take this path to reach the end of a village street in Aldbury, then follow this street straight on past the ´Valiant Trooper´ to the picturesque village green with its pond, ancient stocks, seventeenth-century manor house and a number of attractive cottages.

Joining the reverse direction of Walk 12 take Stocks Road straight on past the green and the ´Greyhound` and out of the village. Some 200 yards beyond its last cottage, having rounded a left-hand bend, turn right onto path AB33 up some steps, through a hedge gap and over a stile and follow a left-hand hedge uphill for some 50 yards until you reach a kissing-gate in it. Turn left through this, then (leaving Walk 12 again) take path AB32 bearing half right across a field to a stile into a wood some distance to the right of an imposing house on the hillside called Little Stocks. Inside the wood, take a path straight on, ignoring two crossing paths and climbing steeply to reach a T-junction of paths near a cottage. Here turn right onto bridleway AB29, keeping right at a fork and soon entering a small clearing. At the far side of the clearing bear slightly left, disregarding a crossing bridleway and continuing through beechwoods to emerge in a clearing by the Bridgewater Monument, erected in 1832 in memory of the third Duke of Bridgewater (1736 - 1803), ´the Father of the English canal system`. This monument stands at the end of a 1.5-mile-long avenue known as Prince´s Riding which was laid out in about 1760 as part of Ashridge Park and the house, rebuilt by James Wyatt and Sir Jeffry Wyatville between 1803 and 1820, can just be seen at the other end.

By the monument, turn right along the edge of the clearing to join a stony track (bridleway AB20). Bear slightly right onto this, reentering the woods, ignoring a lesser fork to the left and passing through a clearing planted with young trees. On entering mature woodland, ignore a branching bridleway to the right and a crossing path, then, at a fork, go right onto bridleway AB26, a sunken track dropping through beechwoods towards Aldbury. After about 100 yards, join bridleway AB21 which merges from your left, then after a further 140 yards, at a path junction with a steep chalk face to your left, bear half left onto bridleway AB11a, a gently rising sunken path which soon enters an ancient yew wood, now with a fence to your right. Where a path commences on top of the right-hand bank of the

54

gully, take this path, keeping parallel to the gully and ignoring a crossing path. Eventually this path leads you to a clearing. At the far end of the clearing, crossing the Chiltern Way, bear left then fork immediately right onto a well-used bridleway into the trees (still ABlla). On reaching a rough drive, continue straight across it and ignore all other crossing tracks until you reach the macadam road across Aldbury Common.

Cross this road and take well-used bridleway ABlla straight on for a quarter mile, ignoring all crossing paths until a field comes into view to your right. Now, joining the Hertfordshire Way, go straight on for a further quarter mile, after 250 yards keeping left at a fork to reach a fork by a corner of the right-hand field. Here keep right then, at a crossways, leaving the Hertfordshire Way, take bridleway NC32 straight on onto Northchurch Common. Soon the scrub gives way to open grassland and Berkhamsted comes into view ahead. On reaching another area of wooded common, ignore crossing tracks and go straight on into the wooded area. At two successive waymarked junctions by the corner of more grassland, bear half left and take bridleway NC34 straight on along the edge of this grassland for over a third of a mile, passing through a dip where Northchurch can be seen to your right and reaching another rise. About 100 yards before the far end of the grassland, at a waymarked junction by a small oak tree, turn right onto a mown grassy track through the bracken (still NC34) and follow it downhill ignoring all crossing tracks. After crossing a flint track, you start climbing again and soon reach the B4506. Cross this road and take bridleway NC34 straight on over the top of a hill, ignoring a branching bridleway to your left and descending to reach scrubland. Here, at a fork, keep right, crossing a macadam drive and eventually reaching the grassy clearing by the B4506 at your starting point.

WALK 10:   Tring

Length of Walk: 6.8 miles / 11.0 Km
Starting Point: 'Rose and Crown Hotel`, Tring.
Grid Ref: SP925114
Maps: OS Landranger Sheet 165
OS Explorer Sheet 181 (or old Sheet 2)
Chiltern Society FP Map No. 18
Parking: Public car park on the north side of Tring High Street just east of Tring Church.
Notes: Heavy nettle growth may be encountered in places in the summer months.

Tring, situated at a gap in the Chiltern escarpment, has always been a place of some importance as it straddles Akeman Street, a Roman road from London to Cirencester, near its junction with the Ancient British Upper Icknield Way which itself passes through the suburbs of the town. In more modern times, Tring has also found itself on the routes of various generations of main traffic arteries in the form of the A41 trunk road from London to Aylesbury and Birmingham, the Grand Union Canal from London to the Midlands and the West Coast main line from Euston to Birmingham and the North. The town boasts a principally fifteenth-century church with a Grinling Gibbons monument to Sir William Gore dating from 1707. Not far from the town centre is a large mansion called Tring Park, originally designed by Sir Christopher Wren. This house, reputedly often visited in its early years by Nell Gwynne, was for two centuries the home of the family of Sir William Gore, the first Director of the Bank of England. It was later acquired by the Rothschilds, who enlarged the house giving it its Victorian appearance. The surrounding park, once noted for its tranquillity, was desecrated in the 1970s by the building of the Tring Bypass which severs the house from the bulk of the park, but if one can ignore the traffic, it remains a place of beauty.

The walk takes you from Tring through Tring Park and across the bypass, then climbs the wooded escarpment to reach Wigginton. It then skirts the village and continues towards Hastoe, then later follows an ancient earthwork known as Grim's Ditch across the plateau into Buckinghamshire before descending through beech-woods to the isolated hamlet of Hang Hill and returning to Tring.

Starting from the 'Rose and Crown Hotel' opposite Tring Church, take the High Street westwards for about 50 yards. Just before a zebra crossing, turn left into a narrow alleyway (path TU37). At a T-junction of paths, turn left, soon turning right again to resume your previous direction, then go straight on to reach Park Street opposite one of the lodges of Tring Park. Cross this road bearing slightly right and take fenced macadam path TU19 to a spiralled footbridge over the A41 into Tring Park. At the far end of the bridge, go through a kissing-gate onto worn path TU21 following the bypass fence straight on, then after a few yards, bearing half right across the outer part of the park, later with views over your left shoulder of Tring Park House. On reaching a gate and kissing-gate into Park Wood, ignore a branching path to your right and turn left through the kissing-gate, taking a flint track, disregarding two branching paths to your right and continuing uphill through the wood on path TU22 to an obelisk. Legend has it that this obelisk was erected by Charles II in memory of Nell Gwynne, but, as he died first, this seems unlikely.

Just before the obelisk, turn right, crossing another track and taking a narrower path (still TU22) steeply uphill. At the top at a junction of tracks and paths, briefly joining the Ridgeway, bear half left onto path TU21, soon reaching a gate and motorcycle trap by a house. Go through the motorcycle trap, then, leaving the Ridgeway, turn right onto enclosed path TU80. Now follow a left-hand hedge straight on along the edge of the wood, ignoring branching paths to the right and garden entrances to the left and at one point passing through a squeeze-stile. On reaching a crossing macadam drive, go straight on, passing through another squeeze-stile and continuing between garden fences, later turning right and eventually reaching the edge of a field. Here turn left onto a fenced path leading to a hedge gap at the far end of the adjoining field into a macadam lane on the edge of Wigginton.

Turn right into this lane (path TU18) and follow it across the upland plateau for over three-quarters of a mile, passing Wick Farm and a gate, later on a gravel track, eventually reaching a macadam road near a road junction at Hastoe, the highest village in Hertfordshire. Turn left onto this road and follow it for a quarter mile. Where a left-hand wood ends and a right-hand wood called High Scrubs begins, joining the Chiltern Way, turn right through a fence gap into High Scrubs, then fork right onto path TU14. This path follows Grim's Ditch, an ancient earthwork of unknown origin clearly visible to your right, straight on through the wood for a quarter mile, then goes straight across a field to a hedge gap ahead. Here cross a rough lane called Brown's Lane and go straight on through another hedge gap. Now follow the left side of a belt of trees concealing Grim's Ditch to the far end of the field. Here, leaving the

Chiltern Way, turn right onto path TU16 through the tree belt crossing Grim's Ditch. On entering another field, go straight on for a few yards to the beginning of another tree belt, then turn left through a hedge gap onto path TU17 following a left-hand hedge to a stile and gate onto a road called Shire Lane which forms the boundary between Hertfordshire and Buckinghamshire.

Turn left onto this road and after some 60 yards, opposite Longcroft farmhouse, turn right onto bridleway CY7, a macadam farm road. Take this straight on for a third of a mile passing a few houses and some farm buildings in a hollow. At the top of the next rise, turn right over a stile onto path B25 and go straight across a large arable field to enter the distant Pavis Wood near where a hedge to the right reaches it. Inside the wood, take path DB27 generally straight on, soon crossing the heavily-used Ridgeway and following a defined path downhill through a plantation. On entering mature woodland, the path joins a sunken gully and follows it downhill through the wood to the valley bottom.

At the bottom of the hill, by a Buckinghamshire County Council noticeboard, turn sharp left onto bridleway DB28 following the inside edge of the wood along the valley bottom. After 250 yards at a fork go straight on, then, at a T-junction in a corner of the wood, turn right onto hedged path B22. Take this path straight on for a quarter mile. Where it starts to swing perceptibly to the left, at a waymarked junction, turn right onto path B19 passing through a hedge gap into a field. Now follow the left-hand field edge straight on, later with an enclosing fence to your right. At the far end of the field, turn right over a stile onto path B20, then bear slightly right across the field to another stile leading to a gap between the corner of a fence and the end of a hedge. Go though this gap and take path DB22 following the left-hand fence past some attractive thatched cottages to cross a stile in the corner of the field, then descend through a hedge gap into a narrow road at Hang Hill.

Turn left along this road passing the thatched cottages. Opposite Hang Hill Cottage, turn right through a gate onto path DB25 following a right-hand hedge to the far end of the field. Here take path DB24 straight on, crossing a stile and passing through a hedge gap. Now turn right and follow the right-hand hedge around the bottom of a field past some cottages. Where the hedge turns right, follow it to a hedge gap onto a road at Terrier's End. Turn left onto this road and follow it to a sharp left-hand bend. Here leave the road and take path DB31 through a gate right of a telephone pole straight on into a field, then go straight on over a rise to a gate right of an ash tree into a hedged lane (byway TU36). Turn left into this lane, reentering Hertfordshire, then turn immediately right into another

58

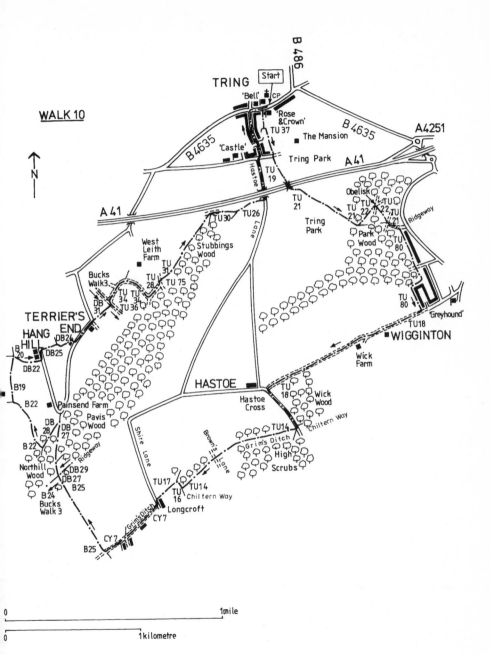

WALK 10

0 _____ 1mile

0 _____ 1kilometre

59

hedged lane (byway TU34) which leads you over a rise. Where this lane forks, take the right-hand option and follow this for some 350 yards, swinging right and climbing until you enter Stubbing's Wood.

At a T-junction just inside the wood, turn left onto byway TU28, then at a fork, keep left to reach a junction of tracks by a gate. Here bear slightly right onto path TU31, soon passing through a kissing-gate and following the inside edge of the wood straight on for a third of a mile with views to your left over the Tring Bypass and western part of the town. On nearing the bypass, join path TU30 which merges from your right, then, at a T-junction, turn right onto a grassy track uphill into a field. Here bear left, following the bypass fence over a slight rise, where there are fine views across Tring towards Ivinghoe Beacon, to reach a disused stile. Now take path TU26 straight on beside the bypass fence through two more fields to a concrete track descending to a gate and kissing-gate into Hastoe Lane. Cross this road, then turn left along its footway passing under the A41 and continuing to the edge of Tring. At a T-junction turn right then immediately left into Akeman Street following this past the Tring Zoological Museum to reach the High Street. Here turn right for your starting point.

WALK 11:   Marsworth (Startop´s End)

Length of Walk: 6.7 miles / 10.8 Km
Starting Point: Entrance to Tring Reservoirs Car Park,
                     Startop´s End, Marsworth.
Grid Ref: SP919141
Maps: OS Landranger Sheet 165
          OS Explorer Sheet 181 (or old Sheet 2)
          Chiltern Society FP Map No.18
How to get there / Parking: Startop´s End, 6 miles east of
     Aylesbury, may be reached from the town by taking the A41
     towards Tring for c.4.5 miles, then turning left onto the
     B489 and following it for just over 2 miles to Startop´s End.
     Here just before the ´White Lion` and canal bridge traffic
     lights, turn right into the Tring Reservoirs Car Park.

**Marsworth, with its much-altered twelfth-century church on a
prominent hillock at the foot of the Chilterns, is perhaps best known
today for the Tring Reservoirs immediately to the south of the
village. These were constructed between 1802 and 1839 to supply
water to the Grand Junction Canal (since 1929 called the Grand
Union Canal) and today, as well as being popular with anglers,
they are frequented by many rare species of water birds and have
therefore been designated as a nature reserve. Within the parish are
also the junctions of the main Grand Union Canal (constructed
between 1793 and 1806) and its Wendover and Aylesbury arms.
The latter is noted for its interesting double lock a few yards from
tbe canal junction which takes the canal down into the Vale of
Aylesbury. In the half century between tbe construction of these
canals and the coming of the nearby London & North Western
main railway line, tbe canals, which were the brainchild of the third
Duke of Bridgewater and his engineer friend, James Brindley,
provided tbe major freight link between London and the
industrialised Midlands and North.**

     **The walk, which is of an easy nature, is, indeed, one for the lovers
of water as much of it follows the towpaths of the three canals and
the banks of the reservoirs, including the beautiful tree-lined cutting
near Bulbourne. Fine views can also be obtained in places of the
nearby escarpment and Vale of Aylesbury.**

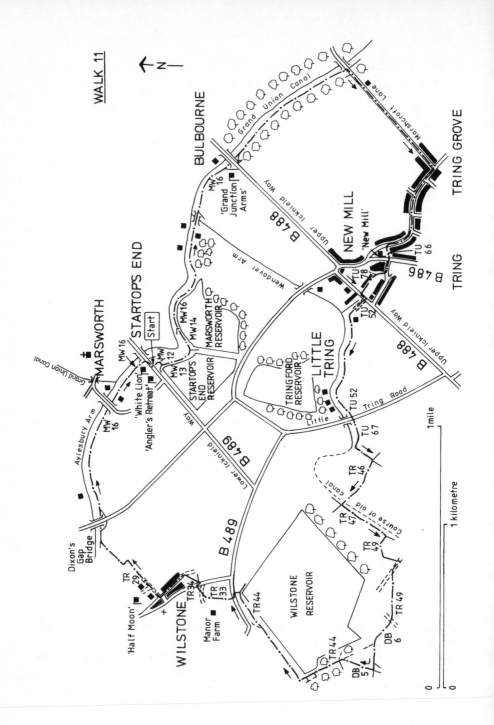

Starting from the entrance to the Tring Reservoirs car park at Startop's End (pronounced 'Starrups'), take path MW12 walking the full length of the car park, then passing through gates and turning right up a flight of steps to reach path MW13 on the banks of Startop's End Reservoir. Turn left onto this, soon joining a gravel path and where the path forks by a causeway separating the Startop's End and Marsworth Reservoirs, fork left, following path MW14 along the top of the bank until it joins the Grand Union Canal towpath (MW16) at Lock No.40. Now take this towpath straight on for 1.3 miles, after half a mile crossing a bridge over the mouth of the Wendover Arm, then passing the canal workshop and 'Grand Junction Arms' at Bulbourne (pronounced 'Booburn') before going under the B488 (Upper Icknield Way) road bridge to enter the beautiful wooded cutting which marks the highest point of the canal. After a further two-thirds of a mile, the path climbs a slope to the Marshcroft Lane bridge where you turn right onto this pleasant, little-used road and follow it for half a mile to its end at Tring Grove on the outskirts of Tring.

Turn right here into Grove Road and follow it for over a third of a mile to a filling station on the left. Now, after a further two houses, turn left onto path TU66, an alleyway between the houses, and follow it to the B486. Cross this road and take New Road straight on. On nearing a right-hand bend, just past the Air Training Corps hut, by a lamp post, turn right onto macadam path TU78, following a left-hand grassy bank concealing a disused canal past a housing estate to your right to reach the B488 (Upper Icknield Way). Turn left onto its pavement, then, having crossed a bridge over the canal, turn right onto path TU52, a macadam drive beside the canal passing a padlocked gate. Where the drive ends at the site of some demolished buildings, follow the canal bank straight on until it joins the Wendover Arm. Now turn left and follow the bank of this restored canal for nearly half a mile to the newly-reconstructed Little Tring Bridge where you climb a flight of steps to Little Tring Road.

Cross the road and take path TU67 down a flight of steps, then continue along a fenced path beside the newly-reexcavated canal for some 200 yards before bearing left to reach a kissing-gate. Go through this, then turn right through a small gate onto path TR46, following a right-hand hedge uphill to gates at the top, where there is a fine view of Wilstone Reservoir ahead. Now go straight on downhill to a kissing-gate into scrubland. Within the scrubland cross a currently dry section of the canal due to be restored to navigation by 2010. Now turn left onto its raised towpath (path TR47). After a quarter mile, turn right down some steps and over a stile onto path TR49, which follows a right-hand fence downhill. At a corner of the field, turn left and follow a right-hand hedge to the next corner. Here go straight on through a hedge gap, then turn right onto a grassy track following a right-hand hedge. Having passed through another hedge gap, bear half left across the next field to a hedge gap left of an ash tree. Here, reentering Bucks, bear half right onto path DB6, following a right-hand hedge to steps leading to a footbridge and stile. Cross these and bear half left across the next field heading towards a stile in the far corner. About 50 yards short of this, turn right onto worn path DB5 crossing the field to a fence gap and footbridge in another corner. Now ignore a stile to your left and a gate to your right and take fenced path TR44 through a belt of trees. On emerging over a footbridge onto the bank of Wilstone Reservoir, follow this for over a quarter mile to a car park to your left at the foot of the embankment. Here descend a flight of steps, then turn right onto a path on the reservoir side of a line of bollards, continuing behind the roadside hedge.

Where this path becomes the footway of the B489 (Lower Icknield Way), cross this ancient road and retrace your steps for 25 yards, then turn right over a concealed stile onto path TR33. Now bear half right across a field to a stile, footbridge and second stile in the far corner. Cross these and a gravel drive, then go straight on through a handgate and across the corner of a field to a concealed footbridge and kissing-gate onto Tring Road. Turn right onto this road, then almost immediately left through a kissing-gate and take path TR34 bearing half left across a field to a further kissing-gate leading to gates at the end of a village street at Wilstone called New Road.

Wilstone, which has only had its own church since 1860, is associated with a story of witchcraft, as in 1751 a suspected witch called Ruth Osborn was hounded by the local populace and murdered by a chimneysweep called Colley who allegedly held her head under water in a local pond. While some say these events took place at nearby Long Marston, what is definitely known is that Colley was hanged for it at Hertford Gaol four months later and his body was brought back and hung in chains at nearby Gubblecote as a warning to local people not to take the law into their own hands.

Follow New Road to Wilstone war memorial, then turn right into Rosebarn Lane. Where its macadam surface narrows and turns left into a housing estate, take path TR29, a grassy lane, straight on to cross a stile, then follow a right-hand hedge straight on to the far end of the field. Here turn left for a few yards, then turn right over a stile and go straight across a field passing left of an electricity pole to reach a stile leading onto the towpath of the Aylesbury Arm of the Grand Union Canal. Turn right onto this towpath and follow it for three-quarters of a mile, going under Dixon's Gap Bridge (if flooded, climbing the bank to a stiled road crossing) and passing four locks with a view of Marsworth Church ahead. At Marsworth the towpath (now path MW16) goes under another bridge, passes a double lock and joins the main Grand Union Canal, then at Startop's End you finally climb a flight of steps by the 'White Lion` to the B489 (Lower Icknield Way) where your starting point is a few yards to the right.

WALK 12:   Pitstone Hill

Length of Walk: (A) 7.4 miles / 11.9 Km
                    (B) 6.5 miles / 10.5 Km
Starting Point: Pitstone Hill car park.
Grid Ref: SP955149
Maps: OS Landranger Sheet 165
          OS Explorer Sheet 181 (or old Sheet 2)
          Chiltern Society FP Map No.19
How to get there / Parking: Pitstone Hill, 3 miles northeast of
     Tring, may be reached from the western end of the town by
     taking the B488 towards Dunstable for 3.7 miles. Just after a
     narrow railway bridge with traffic lights, at a roundabout, go
     straight on, then, at a sharp left-hand bend, take a right turn
     signposted to Aldbury. After nearly half a mile, at the top of
     a rise and opposite a footpath sign, turn right into an
     unmarked car park.
Notes: Heavy nettle growth may be encountered in the summer
     months particularly on paths IV1 and AB50.

Pitstone Hill, near the Buckinghamshire/Hertfordshire boundary,
rising to a height of 715 feet, marks the commencement of the
treeless downs of the northern end of the Chiltern Escarpment which
contrast with the wooded ridges further south. Since the clearance of
encroaching scrub by tbe Chiltern Society in the late 1970s,
regrowth has been controlled by tbe traditional method of sheep-
grazing. Just below tbe hill is the old village of Pitstone, formerly
known as Pightlesthorne, with its fine thirteenth-century church.
Beyond is the village of Pitstone Green which grew considerably to
house workers at the former nearby cement works and is now
joined to Ivinghoe with its magnificent cruciform thirteenth-century
church, fifteenth-century inn, sixteenth-century town hall and other
fine buildings, while in the fields nearer to the hills stands a restored
postmill dating from 1627.

   Both walks first take you along the ridge above these villages,
where superb views abound, with Walk A including an additional
loop to the summit of Ivinghoe Beacon, which, at 756 feet, provides
panoramic views in all directions. Both walks then lead you through
woodland to cross a ridge and descend to the picturesque village of
Aldbury in its sheltered valley, before returning via Aldbury

Nowers and over the crest of Pitstone Hill to your starting point.

Starting from the vehicular entrance to the Pitstone Hill car park, cross the road and take the Ridgeway (path PT8, soon IV27) through a kissing-gate opposite, following a grassy track beside a right-hand fence straight on for a third of a mile until the fence turns right. Here go straight on to the corner of a sporadic hedge, then continue, soon skirting a deep, steep-sided coombe called Incombe Hole to your left and climbing steadily, ignoring a waymarked branching path to your right, to reach a gate and stile near the top of Steps Hill. Do **not** cross the stile, but bear slightly left, passing between the edge of the coombe and the fence to reach open downland. Here go straight on to a marker post at the edge of a belt of scrub, then follow the waymarked path through the scrub. On emerging onto open downland with superb views to your left, ignore a stile to your right and follow the right-hand fence straight on downhill to a kissing-gate. Now take an obvious worn path over a rise and down again to a chalky track. Turn left onto this to reach a bend in Beacon Road, then go past a chain opposite.

Here **Walk B** turns right onto path IV1 following a grassy track to cross a stile by a gate. Now read the next paragraph. **Walk A** takes a chalky track (path IV2) straight on to cross a stile by a gate. Now bear half left along a grassy track across a field to near the corner of a fenced cultivated field to your right, then bear slightly left following a worn path steeply uphill to the crest of the ridge where wide views open out with Edlesborough with its prominent fourteenth-century church backed by Totternhoe Knolls ahead and the Dunstable Downs to your right. Here turn left onto path IV30, following the crest of the ridge uphill to a stile. Cross this, ignore a crossing path and go straight on uphill to the summit of the Beacon with its panoramic views. Now turn left onto path IV26, forking left at the top of a steep slope and soon joining path IV25. After a third of a mile you cross your outward route and follow a chalky path straight on, then, just past a clump of hawthorn bushes to your left, turn left over a stile by a gate onto path IV1.

Here **Walks A and B** take path IV1, following a right-hand fence straight on through two fields crossing two more stiles. Now keep straight on, ignoring a crossing path and passing right of a clump of hawthorn bushes, to reach a gate and kissing-gate into a wood called The Coombe. In the wood, follow a wide grassy track straight on for a quarter mile, then, at a T-junction of tracks, bear half left, soon entering a cypress plantation. Go straight on through this plantation, then, having passed the corner of a left-hand field, keep left at a fork and follow a high wire-mesh fence straight on uphill to the corner of another field to your left. Here ignore a wooden horse-jump into the field and continue along the inside edge of the wood to emerge into a farm storage area. Now follow a left-hand fence straight on past a pond, then, by a gate, turn right onto path IV19, taking an obvious track straight on between farm buildings into a farmyard. Here bear left, then right onto a concrete farm road and follow this for a quarter mile to reach Beacon Road.

Go straight on across this road, bearing half right onto path IV13 into a wood called Duncombe Terrace. Just inside the wood, turn right onto a crossing track, then, at a fork, go left. At a T-junction by a twin-trunked tree, turn left onto a wider track and follow it downhill to reach a major crossing track. Here keep straight on downhill. In the bottom of the dip, ignore a crossing path and go straight on uphill to a stile into a field corner. Cross this and follow the outside edge of the wood straight on. By a corner of the wood, cross a stile and continue to follow its outside edge downhill with fine views towards Aldbury ahead. Where the edge of the wood begins to bear away to the right, leave it, bearing slightly left across the field and passing just left of an electricity and a telephone pole to reach the end of a road at Barley End by the gate to Duncombe Farm.

Cross this road and go through a gap by a stile opposite onto path PT11, bearing half left across a field to a concealed gap in the next hedge. Now go straight across the next field towards a gate at the Hertfordshire boundary. Here ignore a crossing track and go through a kissing-gate beside the gate, then take path AB33 following a right-hand fence to cross a stile by a gate. Now follow a left-hand fence to a gate and stile, then take a drive straight on past a house to a road. Here go straight on through a kissing-gate and across a field to pass through a kissing-gate under the tallest tree in the next hedge (where you join the reverse direction of Walk 9). Now turn right and follow the right-hand hedge to a corner of the field where you cross a stile and descend steps onto Stocks Road - BEWARE BLIND BEND - LISTEN FOR TRAFFIC! Turn left onto this road and follow it into the picturesque village of Aldbury .

On reaching the village centre, where the road forks, keep right (leaving Walk 9) passing the ´Greyhound`, the village pond and seventeenth-century timbered manor house and the village green with its ancient wooden stocks which were in use till the 1830s. At a T-junction, joining the Hertfordshire Way, turn right into Station Road leaving the green and passing the fourteenth-century church where the novelist, Mrs Humphry Ward, niece of Matthew Arnold and aunt of Aldous and Julian Huxley, who lived at Stocks House, was buried in 1920. Just past the church, turn right through a kissing-gate by a gate onto path AB50 and go straight across a field to a gate and stile.

68

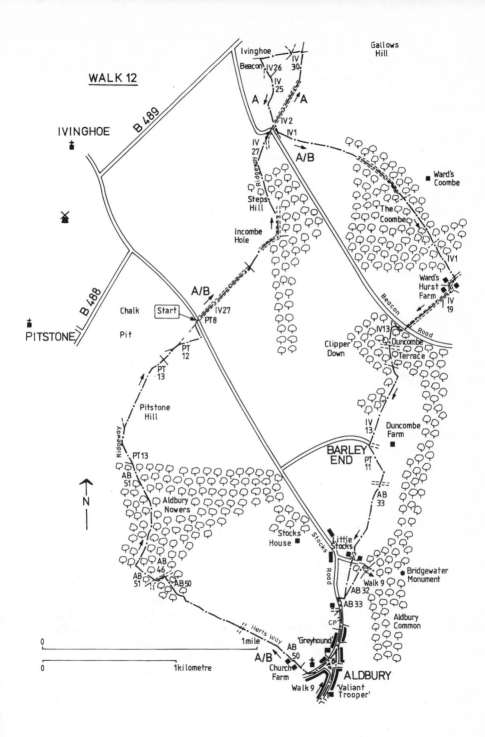

WALK 12

Ivinghoe Beacon

Gallows Hill

B 489

IVINGHOE

IV 26
IV 30
IV 25

A

A

IV2

IV1

Ward's Coombe

IV 27

Ridgeway

A/B

Steps Hill

The Coombe

Incombe Hole

IV1

B 488

PITSTONE

Chalk

Pit

Ward's Hurst Farm

IV 19

Start

A/B

IV27

PT 8

Beacon Road

IV13

Duncombe Terrace

PT 12

Clipper Down

PT 13

Pitstone Hill

Ridgeway

PT13

IV 13

Duncombe Farm

AB 51

BARLEY END

PT 11

N

Aldbury Nowers

AB 33

AB 51

AB 46

Stocks House

Little Stocks

Stocks Road

Bridgewater Monument

AB 50

Walk 9

AB 32

AB 33

Aldbury Common

CP

0 .... 1mile

A/B

'Greyhound'

AB 50

Church Farm

0 .... 1kilometre

Walk 9

Herts Way

ALDBURY

'Valiant Trooper'

69

Cross the stile, then keep straight on to a kissing-gate by the corner of a modern barn at Church Farm. Now follow a path between the barn and a hedge until you emerge through a kissing-gate onto a crossing track. Ignore this track and keep straight on through a further kissing-gate into a fenced path beside a right-hand hedge climbing gently to a kissing-gate onto a crossing bridleway. Cross this and a stile virtually opposite onto a golf course, then take a gravel path, later a mown grass path, straight on to reach a hedge gap. Now follow a right-hand hedge straight on to a stile onto another crossing bridleway. Leaving the Hertfordshire Way, cross the stile and the bridleway, then continue through a concealed kissing-gate into a wood and follow an obvious winding path until you reach a sunken way (path AB46). Turn left onto this and after about 40 yards, turn right onto path AB51 (rejoining the Ridgeway).

Now follow its obvious waymarked course for two-thirds of a mile through a mixture of woodland and scrubland on Aldbury Nowers with fine views to your left across the Tring Gap in places, until a kissing gate at the county boundary leads you out onto the open downland of Pitstone Hill. Here take bridleway PT13, continuing to follow an ancient earthwork which you have been following for some distance, to the top of Pitstone Hill. Where the earthwork bears left, leave it and continue uphill to a marker post by an elderbush, then take a wide grassy track straight on along the ridge towards Ivinghoe Beacon, later dropping, bearing slightly right and ignoring a signposted crossing path. On reaching a crossing sunken gully, fork right onto bridleway PT12, following a right-hand fence to a bridlegate into a picnic area where you turn left for the car park.

WALK 13: Aldbury Common

Length of Walk: 7.1 miles / 11.4 Km
Starting Point: Bridgewater Monument turning off B4506 at
Aldbury Common.
Grid Ref: SP979128
Maps: OS Landranger Sheets 165 & 166
OS Explorer Sheet 181
Chiltern Society FP Map No.19
How to get there / Parking: The starting point, 3 miles north of
Berkhamsted, may be reached from the town by taking the
A4251 to Northchurch, then turning right onto the B4506
and following it for 2.7 miles. About two-thirds of a mile
past the Aldbury turn, turn left onto the macadam road to
the Ashridge Visitor Centre and Bridgewater Monument and
park as soon as possible.
Notes: Heavy nettle growth may be encountered in summer
particularly on parts of path LG7 and bridleway LG10.

Aldbury Common is one of a belt of several mostly wooded
commons extending from the outskirts of Berkhamsted to Aldbury
village and across the Bucks boundary to the Chiltern escarpment.
When the Ashridge Estate was sold in 1929, a large area of these
commons was acquired by the National Trust which has done much
to facilitate public access. Ashridge House, which can be seen at the
eastern end of Prince's Riding (where the car park is located), was
commissioned by the third Duke of Bridgewater before his death in
1803 to replace a mediæval house which had formerly been a
monastery. Designed in the neo-Gothic style by James Wyatt and
his nephew, Sir Jeffry Wyatville, the house was completed in about
1820. At the other end of the Riding, which forms part of the
landscaping carried out by Capability Brown and amended by
Repton, is the Bridgewater Monument erected in 1832 in memory of
the third Duke of Bridgewater who is noted as the 'Father of the
English canal system'.
The walk first explores parts of the wooded Aldbury and
Berkhamsted Commons before crossing Golden Valley to the south-
eastern end of Little Gaddesden. From here, it takes you across a
small valley to Hudnall Common, another National Trust property,
then downhill to tbe Bedfordshire boundary in the Gade valley,

71

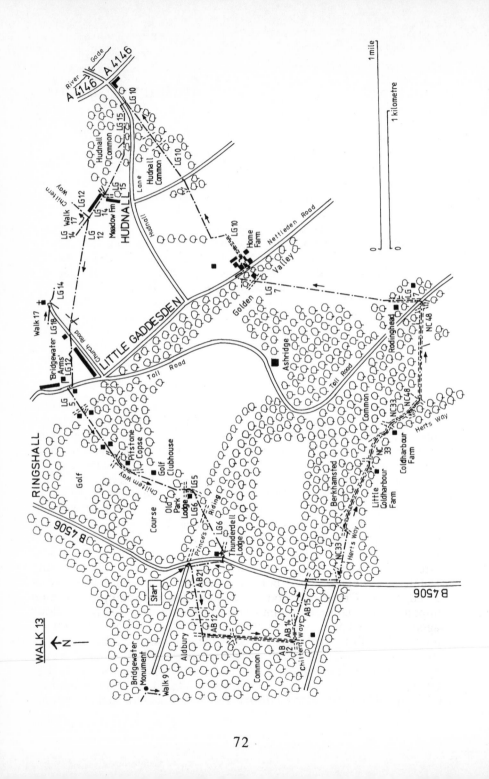

WALK 13

RINGSHALL

HUDNALL

LITTLE GADDESDEN

1 mile

1 kilometre

72

before returning via the north-western end of Little Gaddesden and Ashridge Golf Course to your starting point.

Starting from the entrance to the road to the Bridgewater Monument, take the B4506 southwards for a few yards, then turn right onto bridleway AB21, a grassy path into the woods. Follow it straight on for a third of a mile, ignoring four crossing paths. On reaching a wide crossing track with a wooden junction marker post (path AB12), turn left onto it. At a five-way track junction go straight on, at one point passing a field to your left. Just before a left-hand pond, turn left onto a crossing track (bridleway AB14), briefly joining the Chiltern Way. After about 100 yards at a fork, leaving the Chiltern Way again, take the waymarked right-hand lesser alternative (path AB15) and follow it straight on, passing left of some large beech trees, to reach the B4506.

Cross this road and turn right onto its walkable verge to reach a road junction. Here, joining the Hertfordshire Way, turn left onto bridleway NC33, a rough track into a large clearing. Now bear left and then right to pass a marker post in its far left-hand corner, then take an obvious waymarked track straight on through the woods for half a mile ignoring a crossing track and a track merging from your left. Just past Little Coldharbour Farm, join a stony track and follow it straight on to a track junction by Coldharbour Farm. Here bear slightly right, crossing a track leading to the farm and taking a rough bridle track straight on into the woods. At a fork at the bottom of a slope, leaving the Hertfordshire Way, take the middle option (bridleway NC48), bearing half left and following this track out to the edge of a field. Here bear half left again and follow the outside edge of the woods for nearly half a mile to a corner of the field then go straight on through woodland to reach the Ashridge road.

Cross this road and take path LG7, a macadam drive opposite. Follow this uphill, ignoring a right-hand fork, until you reach a house called Rodinghead. Here leave the drive and take a fenced track straight on between fields to cross a stile by a gate. Now go straight on downhill across a large field heading for and passing through a clump of trees. Here keep straight on downhill into Golden Valley passing through a bridlegate at one point and heading for a tall beech tree at the edge of Cromer Wood left of a fenced pumping station compound. Go straight on into the wood, climbing the steep slope diagonally until you reach an old iron gatepost at the corner of a wall. Now take a sunken path uphill beside the wall through laurel bushes to reach Nettleden Road at Little Gaddesden.

Cross this road and turn right onto its pavement. Just past Shepherd´s Cottage, turn left through white gates onto bridleway LG10 into Home Farm. By the farmhouse gates, bear slightly left off

73

the concrete drive into a narrow bridleway leading between a fence and a wall to a bridlegate. Now turn right then immediately left round the end of a stable block, then go straight on through the left-hand of two gates leaving the farm and taking a fenced track downhill. In the valley bottom, do **not** go through the gate ahead, but turn left and follow the fenced bridleway to the corner of the right-hand field. Here turn right and climb a hill to enter a copse at the edge of Hudnall Common, then keep straight on through the copse to reach a road. Now take bridleway LG10 straight on across open common, with views across the Gade valley towards Studham ahead, heading for a single oak then continuing straight on to reach a well-worn track into scrubland. Take this track straight on downhill through the scrub. After a quarter mile, at a fork bear left to join Hudnall Lane near the Bedfordshire boundary.

Cross this road and take path LG15 opposite, turning left alongside the road and gradually bearing away from it through scrubland. At a fork, keep left, soon emerging onto open common. Bear slightly right across the common to the far right-hand corner, then take a path straight on through a narrow strip of woodland to an access road to houses along the edge of the common. Bear slightly right onto this road (path LG14) and at a right-hand bend by the entrance to Meadow Farm, fork left onto a signposted path between hedges to a kissing-gate into a field, then follow the right-hand hedge straight on to cross a stile (where you meet the route of Walk 17 and join the Chiltern Way). Here take path LG12 bearing half left across a large field, passing right of an oak tree to reach a stile about 80 yards right of the far corner. Now go straight on to a kissing-gate just right of the corner of the next field, then bear half left across a further field to a kissing-gate onto Church Road, which leads to Little Gaddesden´s fifteenth-century church (described in Walk 17). Bear slightly left across this road and a stile, then bear half left across a paddock, passing the rear corner of a garden to reach a kissing-gate near the far corner of the paddock. Go through this and follow a narrow fenced path round the backs of gardens then diagonally across a field to another kissing-gate in front of a red-roofed house onto a road at Little Gaddesden.

Go through this and turn right onto the road, then immediately left onto path LG5 through the ´Bridgewater Arms` car park to a stile in its rear fence. Now follow a fenced path downhill to a macadam access road. Cross this and bear slightly left into a hedged path, soon crossing a further drive and continuing straight on until you enter a wood. Here go straight on uphill, soon passing between golf tees and crossing a track, then keep straight on through woodland and between garden fences to reach a macadam drive. Now keep straight on

74

through the trees to a junction of macadam drives, then bear slightly left and follow one of them past a bungalow called Pitstone Copse. Just past the far end of its garden, by a signpost, leave the drive and bear slightly right onto a grassy track through the trees onto the golf course, then bear slightly left following the edge of the left-hand copse. Now continue straight on between the clubhouse and several greens to a worn track leading uphill through woodland ahead into a former farmyard. On reaching a track junction by Old Park Lodge, bear slightly left passing left of the house, soon on a macadam drive. By the far end of its garden, bear half right onto path LG6 leaving the track and the Chiltern Way and crossing the golf course diagonally, passing right of a green and aiming for a single young oak tree at the edge of the fairway. Here keep straight on into a belt of trees, passing just right of four tall oak trees to reach Prince's Riding, which gives you a brief glimpse to your left of Ashridge House. Cross this ride and take a woodland path straight on, eventually passing the left-hand end of a wooden fence and emerging onto a macadam drive. Turn right onto this and follow it to a gateway by Thunderdell Lodge onto the B4506. Cross this and turn right onto a rough path along its verge back to your starting point.

WALK 14: Piccott´s End

Length of Walk: (A) 8.8 miles / 14.2 Km
(B) 6.2 miles / 10.0 Km
(C) 5.0 miles / 8.0 Km
Starting Point: (A/B) Unmarked car park in Dodds Lane, Piccott´s End.
(C) Corner Farm road junction, Gaddesden Row.
Grid Ref: (A/B) TL052095
(C) TL066117
Maps: OS Landranger Sheet 166
OS Explorer Sheet 182
Chiltern Society FP Maps Nos. 20 (all) & 27 (Walks A/C only)

How to get there / Parking: **(A/B)** Piccott´s End, on the northern edge of Hemel Hempstead, may be reached from the town centre by taking the A4146 towards Leighton Buzzard to a roundabout at its junction with the A4147. Here turn right onto the A4147, then, at the next roundabout, turn left into Piccott´s End. Go straight on through the village for half a mile. Where the right-hand houses end, turn right into Dodds Lane and follow it for some 300 yards, then turn left through a hedge gap into a small unmarked car park.
(C) Corner Farm, Gaddesden Row, 3 miles north of Hemel Hempstead, may be reached from the town by taking the A4146 towards Leighton Buzzard to the ´Red Lion` at Water End. Here turn right onto the road signposted to Flamstead and Markyate and follow it for 1.8 miles to a T-junction at Gaddesden Row. Now turn right and follow the road for 0.8 miles to a road junction by Corner Farm, where you can park on the wide grass verges.
Notes: Heavy nettle growth may be encountered in places in summer on all three walks, while bridleway GG42 on Walks A & C may be very muddy in places even in dry weather.

Piccott´s End, on the River Gade, only a mile north of the centre of Hemel Hempstead, is still an attractive village in a relatively unspoilt setting despite the fact that the town´s rapidly expanding housing estates have covered the tops of the hills on either side of the

valley. In 1953, mediæval wall-paintings were discovered in a fifteenth-century cottage in tbe village called Hall House, which also has a priest hide and a mediæval well.

All three alternative walks pass close to Gaddesden Place on the slopes of the Gade valley above Water End. This house was originally built for the Halsey family in 1768 - 1773 by James Wyatt, who later designed Ashridge, but had to be largely rebuilt after a disastrous fire in 1905. In addition, Walks A and C explore the peaceful plateau to the east of the Gade valley, while Walks A and B cross and recross the scenic Gade valley visiting the picturesque hamlet of Water End and exploring the hills to the west.

Walks A and B start from the unmarked car park in Dodds Lane, Piccott´s End, and take path GG55 leading out of the car park up a rough hedged lane, the right-hand hedge of which soon peters out. Where the track turns right across the field, continue along it to the corner of a hedge. Now go through a hedge gap and follow a winding right-hand hedge straight on uphill to cross a stile with views behind of Hemel Hempstead and the Gade valley. Here follow the right-hand hedge straight on, then, where it turns right, go straight on across the field to a stile by a tree in front of the farmhouse at Wood Farm. Do **not** cross this stile, but turn left onto path GG56 crossing the field to an oak tree. Here go straight on, joining the edge of Varney´s Wood and following it, at one point turning left, to double-gates and a stile at a corner of the wood. Cross this stile and continue along the edge of the wood. Where this turns right, follow a field boundary straight on to reach a hedge gap leading to crossing bridleway GG39. For **Walk A** now omit the next paragraph.

Walk B turns left here onto bridleway GG39 and follows its winding course downhill beside a left-hand hedge for a quarter mile to the bottom corner of the field. Now turn right through a hedge gap onto path GG38 and follow a right-hand hedge uphill, eventually with a young plantation to your left. On reaching the edge of a mature wood called Hogstrough Dell, turn left and follow a right-hand hedge uphill to a gap in it. Turn right through this gap and take a grassy track uphill along the edge of the wood, then across the field to some garages. Here turn left onto a stony track which leads you to a road at Briden´s Camp. Turn right onto this winding road and follow it for a third of a mile, passing the ´Crown & Sceptre` and rounding first a sharp left-hand, then a sharp right-hand bend. Some 130 yards beyond the right-hand bend, turn left onto path GG22, the concrete road towards Home Farm. Where its concrete ends, turn left over a stile by double-gates onto path GG21 rejoining **Walk A**. Now omit the next four paragraphs.

Walk A turns right onto bridleway GG39, joining **Walk C**, then **Walks A and C** follow the outside edge of a tree-belt. At the far end of the tree-belt, continue through a hedge gap and follow a left-hand hedge straight on through three fields for nearly a mile with views of the modern outskirts of Hemel Hempstead to your right. Near the far end of the third field, descend into a sunken gully to join Cupid Green Lane at a sharp bend. Now take this narrow road straight on downhill and up again for a quarter mile to reach the Corner Farm road junction at Gaddesden Row.

At the Corner Farm road junction (**the start of Walk C**), **Walks A and C** take the Redbourn road straight on. After about 330 yards, opposite double-gates, turn left onto fenced bridleway GG42, turning right then left then right again. Now continue between fences, turning left by a house and passing a paddock to reach the edge of a wood. Take the bridleway straight on to the far side of the wood, then by a metal gate to your right, take a green lane straight on (joining the reverse: direction of Walk 15), soon passing Long Wood and a field to your left and entering Round Spring Wood. Take the bridleway through the wood, soon transferring through a gap in the right-hand hedge to the other side of the hedge and continuing between it and a fence to Upper Wood Farm.

Here (leaving Walk 15 again) turn left onto a farm road (path GG30) and follow it for a third of a mile to the Gaddesden Row road near the ´Old Chequers`. Turn right onto this road, then, at a junction, turn left onto the Water End and Hemel Hempstead road and follow it for a third of a mile. Just past the bottom of a dip, turn right through a hedge gap onto path GG32 following a right-hand hedge to the far side of the field. Here go straight on into the middle of a crossing avenue of time trees, then turn left onto path GG34, a grassy track along the avenue. Where the track bears left and leaves the avenue, follow it, immediately forking right onto path GG33 along the outside edge of the avenue, then the edge of London Wood. On reaching the gravel road to Home Farm (path GG22), turn left onto it. Just before it becomes concreted, **Walk A** turns right over a stile by double-gates onto path GG21, then omit the next paragraph.

Walk C takes path GG22 straight on along the concrete road, then turns right onto a public road and follows it for a third of a mile. Having passed the ´Crown and Sceptre`, at a sharp right-hand bend, turn left onto path GG38, a stony track beside some farm cottages with a fine view down the Gade valley to Hemel Hempstead. On reaching some garages, turn right onto a grassy track and follow it past a copse to a hedge gap. Go through this gap, then turn left and follow a left-hand hedge downhill through a plantation to a hedge gap. Do **not** go through this gap, but turn right and follow a left-hand hedge downhill to a hedge gap in the bottom corner of the field. Go through this gap, then turn left onto well-worn bridleway GG39, following a right-hand hedge uphill for a quarter mile to rejoin **Walk A** by a belt of trees. Now go back four paragraphs.

Walks A and B now take path GG21 bearing slightly right across parkland with a view to your right of Home Farm (a good example of a technologically advanced Victorian farm) to cross a stile just right of a large oak tree where the imposing façade of Gaddesden Place comes into view ahead. Now keep straight on across two parkland fields to a metal gate right of Gaddesden Place. Here, joining the Chiltern Way, bear slightly left across the next field with fine views to your right over Great Gaddesden and the Gade valley to pass through a further gate, then keep straight on downhill, soon with a close-up view of Gaddesden Place to your left, passing between a conifer and an oak to reach a stile. Now cross the corner of another field to a further stile with a fine view of Water End with its picturesque seventeenth-century brick-and-timber cottages ahead. Here bear slightly left, aiming for an ash tree just left of a cream cottage to reach the corner of a garden fence. Follow the fence straight on past the cottage towards the road to a stile onto the garden path and a handgate leading onto the A4146 at Water End.

Cross this road and turn right, then turn immediately left onto path GG66 leading between garden walls to two stiles. Having crossed these, bear half right, following a fence at first to reach a footbridge over the River Gade. At the far end of this bridge, turn left (still on GG66) and follow the river to a footbridge over a small watercourse, then go straight on, gradually deviating from the river to reach a stile. Cross this and bear slightly right to join a right-hand fence then follow it, ignoring a stile in it, to reach a gate and stile onto Nettleden Road. Turn right onto this road, then after about 60 yards, turn left through a kissing-gate onto path GG63. Now go straight on uphill, passing left of a large tree stump, to reach a track into Heizdin´s Wood. Before entering the wood, turn round for a fine view across the valley, then follow the track uphill through the wood ignoring a crossing path. On leaving the wood, bear half right across a field to the left-hand of two small oak trees, then bear slightly left to reach the end of a hedge. Here bear half left onto path GG62 along the near side of the hedge to a kissing-gate. Go through this, then bear slightly right into a fenced lane leading to Water End Road on the edge of Potten End.

Turn right onto this road and at a right-hand bend, turn left through a small gate onto fenced path GG59. On crossing a stile, follow the sporadic right-hand hedge straight on, then, after about 50 yards, by an oak tree, go through a gap in the hedge and walk downhill between it and a wire fence to a stile at the bottom. Cross this and turn left (now on path HH17), then turn right over a stile by a gate onto a fenced farm track uphill to reach gates at Boxted Farm. Go straight on through the smaller gate and follow a left-hand fence straight on to a kissing-gate leading to the farm drive. Cross this drive and a stile and keep straight on to cross a second drive flanked by stiles, then bear right and follow a left-hand fence to a further stile leading to a farm drive. Turn left onto this, then, at a junction of drives, leaving the Chiltern Way, go straight on through a kissing-gate onto path HH18 and bear half left, following a left-hand fence to a gate and stile. Now bear slightly left and follow a left-hand fence to the far side of the field. By the corner of a hedge, by an ash tree, turn right and follow the left-hand hedge through two fields to Fennycroft Road on the edge of Hemel Hempstead.

Turn left onto this road, then, just past the junction with Parklands, fork left onto an access road leading to a gate and stile. Now cross this stile onto path HH13, following the edge of a field straight on beside gardens. At its far end, cross a stile and continue between a hedge and a fence. Where the fence ends, follow the outside edge of Warnersend Wood, then a right-hand hedge straight on. At the far end of the field, bear slightly right to pass through a squeeze-stile, then continue along a fenced path. On reaching a bend in a track, join it and follow it straight on past a wood and farm buildings to reach a macadam drive, then continue along this, soon reaching the A4146. Cross this road and go straight on across a bridge over the Gade to reach the village street in Piccott's End. Turn left onto this and after some 130 yards, turn right into Dodds Lane. About 30 yards up the lane, where a left-hand hedge begins, leave the road and take path HH10 following the back of the roadside hedge to a hedge gap into the car park.

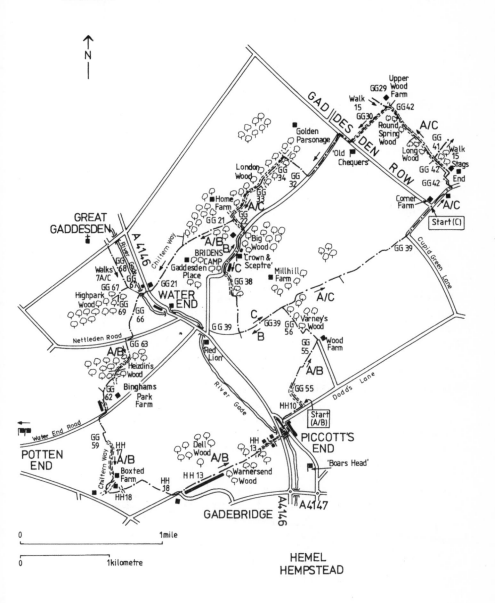

81

WALK 15:   Redbourn

Length of Walk: 9.1 miles / 14.6 Km
Starting Point: Car park near cricket pitch on Redbourn
                      Common.
Grid Ref: TL103119
Maps: OS Landranger Sheet 166
            OS Explorer Sheet 182
            Chiltern Society FP Maps Nos. 20 & 27
How to get there / Parking: Redbourn, 4 miles northeast of
   Hemel Hempstead, may be reached from the town by taking
   the B487. After passing under the M1, turn left onto a road
   signposted to Church End and follow it straight on for half a
   mile to a car park to your left on Redbourn Common.
Notes: Heavy nettle growth may be encountered in the summer
   months, particularly on path FS45, while bridleway GG42
   may be very muddy in places even in dry weather.

**Redbourn in the Ver valley, the name of which means ´reedy
stream` suggesting that the area was once marshy, is set around an
extensive and very attractive common where cricket has been
played since 1666. At the southwestern end of the common is the
original village known as Church End where a street of picturesque
cottages leads to the twelfth-century church, noted for its carved oak
rood screen dating from 1478. East of the common is the village
High Street on the line of a Roman road called Watling Street. This
road, which has now been bypassed by the A5183 (formerly A5),
was particularly busy in the eighteenth and early nineteenth
centuries when it formed the main stagecoach road from London to
Birmingham, Liverpool and Holyhead and thus inns and other
buildings sprang up here during this period to service the coaches.
Before the construction of the M1, the age of the motor-car brought
another flood of heavy traffic to the High Street, but with the bypass
it is now relatively peaceful again. Finally, north of the common is
an area of modern housing estates which have swelled the
population to 6,000, but nevertheless this is only a small development in comparison with what would have occurred if the one-time
plan to make Redbourn the site of a new town had been
implemented.**
    The walk takes you out of Redbourn over the hills to the west of

the Ver valley to the hilltop village of Flamstead. From here, it leads you southwestwards through remote hill country to near the scattered community of Gaddesden Row before returning through equally remote hill country to Redbourn.

Starting from the back of the car park on Redbourn Common, turn right onto macadam path RB17 within a fine avenue of lime trees (briefly interrupted on one side by the cricket pitch) and follow it to Lybury Lane. Turn left onto this road and follow it straight on for over a third of a mile, crossing the common and passing through a housing estate. On reaching an open green in the middle of the estate, turn right onto a road round the edge of the green, then take the first road leaving the green to reach a T-junction. Here turn left into Snatchup, then, at a second T-junction, cross a road called Long Cutt and take hedged path RB51 straight on, ignoring a branching path to the left and following a permissive path straight on through a recreation ground to reach the end of a residential road.

Take this road straight on, then turn right into the first right-hand cul-de-sac. At its far end turn left onto a macadam path, then immediately right onto crossing macadam path RB52. At a further T-junction of paths, turn left onto enclosed path RB3 and follow it straight on for 150 yards, ignoring a branching path to your left and continuing until a hedge forces you to turn left into a field. Now follow a right-hand hedge, almost immediately turning right. Where the hedge ends, ignore a branching path to your right and bear slightly left, following a right-hand fence. Where the fence turns right, go straight on along a grassy path, later passing through a gap in the vestiges of a hedge and following the right-hand side of a line of trees. On reaching a more solid hedge, keep left of this and follow it straight on to the boundary fence of the M1. Here bear half right, following the M1 fence through a wood and a field to Redding Lane.

Turn left onto this road, crossing a bridge over the M1, then just before reaching Norrington End Farm, turn left through a kissing-gate by a gate onto path RB5 and go straight across a field to the left-hand end of a hedge. Here turn right onto path RB3a, soon crossing a stile. then continuing straight on with a fine view of the Ver valley ahead to reach a concealed gate and stile in the left-hand hedge. Cross this stile, then turn right over a second onto path FS23, following the right-hand hedge downhill. Where this hedge turns right, bear slightly left downhill to cross a stile, then follow a right-hand fence straight on to cross two further stiles. Now bear slightly left uphill to a stile under a crab-tree to the right of the top left-hand corner of the field. Do **not** cross this stile, but instead turn left onto path FS24 and follow the right-hand hedge to the corner of the field. Here enter a hedged lane

83

and follow it straight on to Delmerend Lane. Turn right onto this road, then, after about 100 yards, joining the Chiltern Way, turn left onto path FS25, another hedged lane. On emerging through a squeeze-stile into a field, follow the right-hand hedge straight on to a kissing-gate into a fenced alleyway leading to a residential road in Flamstead.

Flamstead, a corruption of 'Verlamstead', is an attractive village set on a hilltop above the Ver valley. The village, when seen from afar, is dominated by its magnificent twelfth-century church with its massive tower containing Roman bricks and its interior boasting some fine mediæval murals and later marble monuments.

Turn right onto this road and follow it round left- and right-hand bends, then turn left through a kissing-gate into the churchyard. Here, if wishing to visit one of the village pubs or look at the attractive village centre, take the right-hand path (FS29) passing right of the church. Otherwise, take path FS30, the left-hand of the three paths through the churchyard, to gates leading to Trowley Hill Road. Turn left onto this road, then immediately right onto path FS32, a fenced alleyway leading you out past a housing estate into a field. Now go straight on across the field, passing an electricity pole and then heading for a hedge gap left of an ash tree in tall bushes ahead. Go through this gap and turn left onto a narrow road called Pietley Hill. At a left-hand bend, turn right through a hedge gap onto path FS37, bearing slightly right downhill to a fence gap at the bottom, then continue uphill to reach the top hedge, where you turn right and follow the near side of the hedge to a rustic stile in a field corner leading to Wood End Lane where there is a fine view behind you across the valley to Flamstead.

Turn right onto this road, then, just after Scratch Wood begins to your left, turn right through a gap by a gate and take path FS45 bearing slightly left across a field to the near corner of a wood called Yewtree Spring. Here keep right of the wood and follow its outside edge to a waymarked fence gap into it. Turn left through this and follow the waymarked path through this wood, carpeted in bluebells in April and May, passing left of an ornamental pond. On leaving the wood, bear slightly right across the field, with views ahead across these remote hills towards the distant Bedfordshire village of Studham, to reach the corner of a hedge, then turn left and follow the hedge to a stile in it. Cross this and turn left, following a left-hand hedge. On nearing Little Woodend Cottages, where the left-hand fence diverges from the hedge, cross a stile in the fence and keep left of a shed to join a drive by the cottages. Take this drive straight on to reach a road then turn left onto it and follow it through Newlands Wood. Just after a slight left-hand bend turn right over a stile onto fenced path FS46

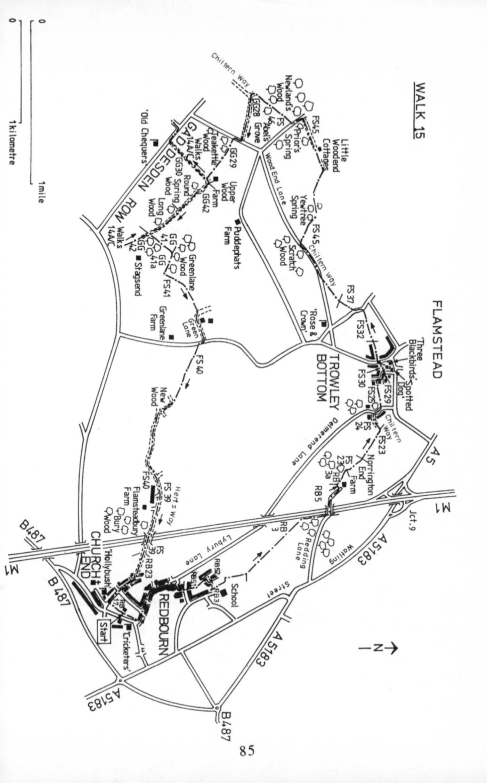

WALK 15

85

leading to a kissing-gate, then bear slightly left across a field passing the corner of a copse called Abel´s Grove to reach gates in the far corner of the field. Here turn left into a green lane and follow it to a right-hand bend, then, leaving the Chiltern Way, turn left through a hedge gap onto path GG28 following a grassy track beside a right-hand hedge for over a quarter mile to a road. Turn right onto this road, then, after about 80 yards, turn left through a hedge gap onto bridleway GG29 following a fenced track beside Teakettle Wood, then a right-hand hedge to Upper Wood Farm.

Here, on reaching a farm road (path GG30), if wanting refreshments, turn right onto it to reach the ´Old Chequers`, Gaddesden Row, in just over a third of a mile. Otherwise, join the reverse direction of Walk 14, crossing the farm road, passing left of the corner of a fence and taking bridleway GG42, a fenced track right of two gates, straight on beside a right-hand hedge. On reaching the corner of Round Spring Wood, follow the track into and through the wood to reach a field. Here take the fenced bridleway straight on beside a left-hand hedge to enter Long Wood, then continue through it and along a hedged lane until you reach the beginning of a third wood left of the lane. Leaving Walk 14, turn left here over a stile by an iron gate onto path GG41, following the outside edge of the wood straight on. Where the edge of the wood turns right, go straight on downhill to reach the edge of Greenlane Wood, then turn right onto path GG41a following it. At the far end of the wood, turn left through a hedge gap onto path FS41 following the outside edge of the wood, then a left-hand hedge uphill. Where the hedge turns left, bear slightly right across the field, heading for farm buildings in the hedge ahead, to reach a hedge gap into Green Lane. Bear slightly right into this appropriately-named lane and follow it passing a cottage to reach a T.junction with a macadam road.

Here turn right and follow the road for some 60 yards. Just past an electicity pole, turn left onto path FS40 following a crop-break, later a hedge, for some 700 yards to reach New Wood. Now join a track and follow it straight on for over half a mile, ignoring all branching tracks and eventually reaching a macadam farm road near Flamsteadbury Farm. Briefly joining the Hertfordshire Way, turn right onto this road (bridleway FS39, later RB23) and follow it past the farm and over the M1 into Redbourn. On reaching the village, take this road called Flamsteadbury Lane straight on to Redbourn Common. Here take West Common straight on, then, just before Church End to your right, turn left onto macadam path RB17 within the avenue of lime trees and follow it back to your starting point.

WALK 16: Markyate

Length of Walk: 4.9 miles / 7.9 Km
Starting Point: ´Sun lnn`, Markyate.
Grid Ref: TL062164
Maps: OS Landranger Sheet 166
OS Explorer Sheet 182
Chiltern Society FP Map No.21
How to get there / Parking: Markyate, 3.5 miles southwest of
Luton, may be reached by leaving the M1 at Junction 9
(Flamstead). Now take the A5 towards Dunstable and fork
left onto the road into the village. On reaching the village
centre, find a suitable on-street parking place in one of the
side-streets.

Markyate, formerly known variously as Markyate Street or even
Market Street, grew up as a long straggle of mainly eighteenth-
century buildings along Watling Street, the Roman road from
Dover via London, Verulamium (St. Albans) and Durocobrivae
(Dunstable) to the West Midlands, and has only in recent years
spread out substantially from this road. Although the village was
bypassed by the modern A5 in 1957, a number of old coaching inns
still bear witness to the fact that the main road used to run through
the village. To the north of Markyate is its Georgian parish church
built in 1724 in a park known as Markyate Cell because it was in
mediæval times the site of a nunnery. The present house with this
name, built in 1825, replaced an earlier one which, in the
seventeenth century, had been the home of a widow named Lady
Katherine Ferrers. Legend has it that she became a highwayman
and later haunted both the old house and the A5. Earlier in the
same century, the village also featured in national events when the
servant of Ambrose Rookwood, one of the conspirators in the
Gunpowder Plot, was arrested at the ´Sun Inn` in 1605. Some 130
years later, Markyate was also the location of a boarding school
attended by the young William Cowper of Berkhamsted who was
later to achieve fame as a poet.
    The walk, which includes some fine views, first takes you out of
Markyate and the Ver valley and explores the hill country on the
Bedfordshire boundary to the north of the village before recrossing
the Ver valley near Kensworth Lynch and following the top of its

CADDINGTON

WALK 16

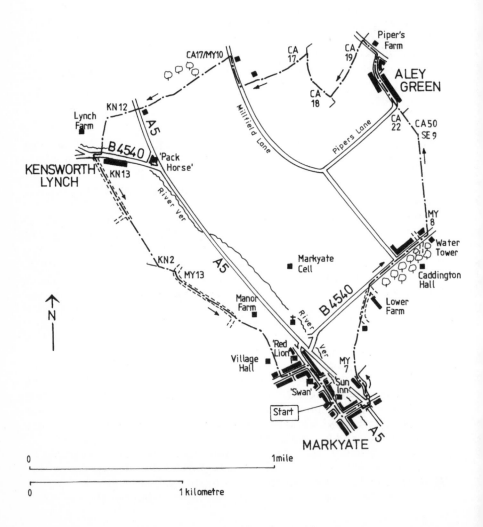

MARKYATE

0   1 mile

0   1 kilometre

88

southern slope to Markyate.

Starting from the ´Sun lnn` in Markyate High Street, follow the High Street southeastwards for about 60 yards, then turn left into Hicks Road and follow it out to the A5. Cross the main road by way of a footbridge and at the far end of it, turn left down a flight of steps and cross the extension of Hicks Road. Now take a macadam road opposite, called The Ridings, straight on to cross a stile by a gate at the far end, then take path MY7, bearing slightly right across a field to cross a stile at the left-hand end of a hedge. Now bear half left across the next field to the near corner of a garden hedge. Keep left of this hedge and follow it straight on, then, where the hedge turns right, continue straight on to join a drive which leads you out to the B4540.

Cross this road, turn right onto its pavement and follow it for a third of a mile, ignoring a side-turning and passing a row of bungalows. Opposite a water-tower in the trees to your right, turn left over a stile onto path MY8 and bear half right across a field, heading between two electricity poles ahead to pass a redundant midfield stile, then continuing towards the distant Caddington Church to cross a stile at the county boundary in the far corner of the field. Here turn left onto path SE9, passing through a kissing-gate, then take path CA50 following a left-hand fence to a handgate at the far side of the field. Pass through this and take a fenced path, ignoring a gap in the left-hand fence and entering a right-hand field. Now take path CA22 following the left-hand hedge straight on to a gate and rails, through which you climb to reach Pipers Lane on the edge of the Bedfordshire village of Aley Green.

Turn right onto this road and follow it through Aley Green to a T-junction by Piper´s Farm. Here turn left and after some 130 yards, turn left again over a footbridge and through a hedge gap onto path CA19, following a right-hand hedge uphill at first then levelling out. On reaching a corner of the field, turn right onto path CA18, following a right-hand hedge through two fields with views of Caddington to your right ahead. At the far end of the second field, do **not** go through the hedge gap, but instead turn left onto path CA17 and follow a right-hand hedge for a third of a mile through a field and a plantation to a gap by gates into Millfield Lane. Turn right onto this road, then, just past a white house, turn left through a gap by a gate onto path CA17/MYl0, following a left-hand hedge to reach a copse. Go straight on through the copse, then continue through scrubland past an oak tree to a gap in the next hedge. Drop down though this gap and go straight on downhill with views across both spurs of the Ver valley ahead to a kissing-gate just left of an ash tree. Now continue straight on downhill to a gate and kissing-gate in the bottom left-hand corner of the field leading to the A5.

Here cross the A5, bearing slightly left to a squeeze-stile opposite the entrance to an industrial site, then take signposted path KN12 through this and straight on uphill across a field to reach a marker post at the hilltop. Now turn left and head for a yellow-topped marker post and a culvert over a ditch, which is all there is of the River Ver near its source at Kensworth Lynch.

Cross this culvert and turn right onto the B4540. After a few yards, turn left through a concealed swing-gate left of double gates onto path KN13, a farm track which climbs steadily, then levels out with fine views of the Ver valley to your left. After joining a left-hand hedge, just past a wooden electricity pylon, turn left through a hedge gap onto path KN2 and bear half right across the corner of a field to reach another hedge gap. Go through this gap and take path MY13 following a grassy track straight on beside a left-hand hedge, with views ahead of Flamstead on a distant hilltop and through gaps in the hedge of the Ver valley including Markyate Cell in its wooded park. At the far end of the field, go through a hedge gap and follow a left-hand hedge straight on beneath a power line past Manor Farm to a kissing-gate at the far end of the field. Go through this gate and follow the left-hand hedge past a recreation ground, the village hall and a children's playground into an alleyway leading to Cavendish Road in Markyate. Turn left onto this road, following it downhill to the High Street, then turn right to reach your starting point.

WALK 17:   Studham

Length of Walk: 6.5 miles / 10.4 Km
Starting Point: Crossroads by 'Red Lion`, Studham.
Grid Ref: TL023158
Maps: OS Landranger Sheets 165 & 166
OS Explorer Sheets 181 (or old Sheet 2) & 182
Chiltern Society FP Maps Nos. 19 & 20
How to get there / Parking: Studham, 4 miles south of
Dunstable, may be reached from the town by taking the
B489 towards Aston Clinton, then forking left onto the
B4541 towards Whipsnade and the Downs and following it
for 2.2 miles to a roundabout at its junction with the B4540.
Here take the Studham and Hemel Hempstead road straight
on for 1.6 miles, then, at a crossroads in the village by the
village hall, 'Red Lion` and war memorial clocktower, there
is a small car park on the left. If full, turn right into Church
Road and find a suitable on-street parking place.
Notes: Heavy nettle growth may be encountered in places in the
summer months.

Studham, the southernmost village in Bedfordshire, nestles in a
hollow in the backland of the Dunstable Downs, surrounded by an
extensive upland plateau. Until 1897, the village, which was once a
centre of the straw-plait industry and was one of the early
strongholds of Nonconformity, in fact, straddled the Hertfordshire
boundary and it was only then that the southern half of its extensive
common and many of its scattered farms and cottages were
transferred to the same county as the church and village centre. The
cement-rendered thirteenth-century church, which is somewhat
isolated and hidden at the end of its cul-de-sac lane, has a
surprisingly beautiful interior with fine carved stone capitals and an
unusual carved Norman font pre-dating the present building.
    The walk, which traverses three counties, leads you first west-
wards across the plateau past the church to descend the escarpment
to the Buckinghamshire village of Dagnall, before turning south and
climbing through quiet woodland to the hilltop Hertfordshire village
of Little Gaddesden. You then return northeastwards to Studham,
on the way skirting Hudnall and crossing the upper reaches of the
Gade Valley. Although basically an open walk with fine viewpoints,

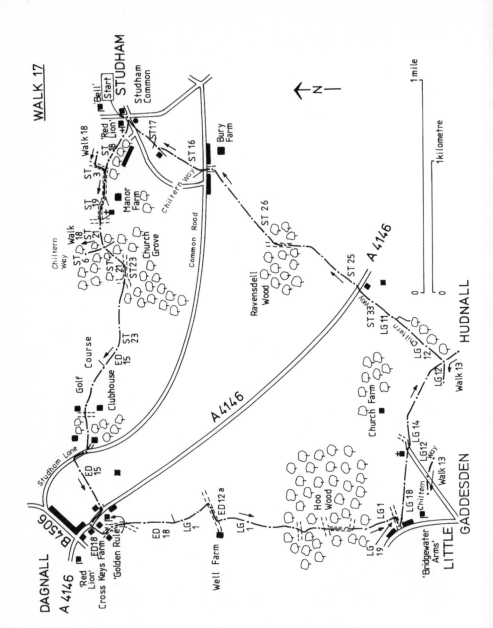

some pleasant woodland provides variety.

Starting from the crossroads by the ʹRed Lionʹ at Studham, take Church Road, then turn right onto path ST18 striking off between Studham Methodist Church and a road called Swannellʹs Wood. Now go through a gap by a gate and follow a left-hand hedge through two fields, joining Walk 18 in the second field. At the far end of this field, take path ST19 following a grassy track which bears half right to the corner of a hedge and tree belt concealing Studham churchyard then bears half left and follows the churchyard hedge to a crossing track. Here take path ST21 straight on over a stile, following a right-hand fence past two large trees, then bear slightly left diverging gradually from the fence to reach a stile and footbridge into a wood called Church Grove.

Inside the wood, disregard a crossing bridleway (the Chiltern Way, onto which Walk 18 turns right) and follow a well-defined track straight on until you reach a waymarked T-junction. Here turn right onto path ST23 and follow this track to a crossing track at the edge of the wood. Now go straight on, leaving the wood by a gap to the right of the horse-jump ahead. Follow the edge of the wood, later a left-hand hedge, straight on to a hedge gap at the far end of the field. Go through this and bear slightly right across the next field to a concealed hedge gap just beyond a slight kink in the right-hand hedge. Go through this gap onto Buckinghamshire path ED15, then bear slightly right across a golf course, keeping right of a green and fairway ahead to reach a marker post in the trees ahead. Here ignore a branching path to your right and bear slightly left following the left-hand edge of a tree belt. At the far end of this tree belt, bear slightly left, passing left of a tee and a row of conifers to reach the right-hand end of a short section of hedge, then go straight on, crossing a tee to reach a hedge gap at the near right-hand corner of a wood leading to a stile. Here follow a fenced path straight on downhill, ignoring a crossing drive and continuing for some 350 yards to a stile. Cross this and follow a right-hand fence beside a drive to a handgate leading into Studham Lane. Turn right onto this road, then, shortly after a left-hand bend, turn left over a stile onto fenced path ED15, leading downhill to a car park and the A4146 at Dagnall.

Turn right onto this road, passing the ʹGolden Ruleʹ. Just past Cross Keys Farm on the left, turn left through a gate onto path ED18, passing left of a building and bearing slightly left to a gate at the left-hand end of a hedge leading to a farmyard. Here go straight on past some farm buildings. Near the back of the farm by a wooden building with an electricity pole in front of it, turn left onto a track, between the buildings. Follow it, bearing slightly right out of the farm and through a hedge gap, then beside a left-hand hedge. Where the track turns right, leave it and bear slightly right across the field to its far corner. Here bear slightly left onto Hertfordshire bridleway LG1, crossing the next field to the corner of a hedge. Now bear left of the hedge and follow it to a track junction. Here turn right (soon on bridleway ED12a), heading towards Well Farm until you reach a left-hand hedge gap. Turn left through this, keeping left of a fence and swinging right beside a right-hand hedge (soon on bridleway LG1 again). Where the hedge ends, go straight on across a field to a bridlegate. Go through this gate, then bear slightly left across a field to a bridlegate into Hoo Wood.

Inside the wood, follow the obvious bridleway straight on uphill, ignoring all crossing tracks until, after more than a third of a mile, you reach a bridlegate into a field. Here follow the right-hand hedge straight on across the field to a gate and bridlegate. Go through the bridlegate and turn right onto LG19, following a right-hand hedge to a gate and kissing-gate onto a road at Little Gaddesden. Do **not** go through these, but turn sharp left onto path LG18 doubling back across two paddocks to cross two stiles, then keep straight on across the next field to the corner of a fence by a lightning-damaged oak tree. Follow this right-hand fence straight on to a kissing-gate, from which the fifteenth-century church comes into view ahead.

This church is principally notable for the wealth of memorials which it contains to members of the Egerton family, the Earls and Dukes of Bridgewater, who held nearby Ashridge Park from 1604 to 1849, including one to the third and last Duke who inspired the construction of the Grand Union Canal and is consequently known as 'The Father of British Inland Navigation`.

Now go straight on across a field to pass through two kissing-gates and reach Church Road, then follow this straight on past the church to a stile opposite the second gate into the churchyard. Turn right over this, then immediately left onto path LG14, following a left-hand fence to cross a stile. Now bear slightly left across a field to a concealed stile in the hedge ahead. Cross this and follow a left-hand hedge straight on for a third of a mile to a stile near an oak tree, where you meet but do not join the route of Walk 13. Do **not** cross this stile, but instead, joining the Chiltern Way, turn left through a hedge gap onto path LG12 and follow a right-hand hedge downhill through two fields (later on bridleway LG11, then bridleway ST33) to reach the A4146 in the Gade valley above the source of its river.

Cross this main road, go through a gap by a gate opposite and take bridleway ST25 following a left-hand hedge uphill. Soon after the hedge bears right, go through the second gap in it and continue uphill between a deer fence protecting a young plantation and a belt of trees with fine views to your left towards Ivinghoe Beacon to reach a gate into Ravensdell Wood. Go through this and follow a track through the wood to another gate, then follow a right-hand hedge for a few yards to a kissing-gate in it. Turn right through this onto path ST26, then bear half left across a large field, heading towards some distant houses on the edge of Studham to reach a kissing-gate. Now bear slightly right across the next field to a gate and kissing-gate left of a large red-brick house leading into a lane. Follow this lane out to Common Road and cross this, bearing half right to a hedge gap. Go through this and leaving the Chiltern Way, take path ST16, bearing half right across a field, following what is normally a crop break to the right-hand corner of a large house ahead which was formerly the village school. Here bear right through a gap onto Studham Common, following bridleway ST17 along the valley bottom, then through a belt of scrub. On emerging onto open common by a football pitch, bear left to meet Church Road opposite the Methodist Church, then turn right onto this road for your starting point.

WALK 18:   Whipsnade Downs

Length of Walk: (A) 6.8 miles / 10.9 Km
                        (B) 2.5 miles / 4.0 Km
Starting Point: Bison Hill National Trust car park, Whipsnade
                        Downs.
Grid Ref: TL000184
Maps: OS Landranger Sheet 166
               OS Explorer Sheet 182
               Chiltern Society FP Map No.21
How to get there / Parking: Whipsnade Downs, 2.5 miles
    southwest of Dunstable, may be reached from the town by
    taking the B489 towards Aston Clinton for 2.5 miles to a
    roundabout. Here turn left onto the B4506 towards Dagnall,
    then, after a quarter mile, turn left again onto the B4540 up
    Whipsnade Downs. Near the top, look out for the signposted
    Bison Hill Car Park on your left.
Notes: Deep mud may be encountered on bridleway WP1 even
    in dry weather, as may heavy nettle growth in the summer
    months.

Whipsnade Downs and nearby Dunstable Downs both provide a
rural playground for nearby built-up areas, the lofty location of
which offers panoramic views over the Ouzel valley and beyond, as
well as a pleasant breeze even on the hottest day. The nearby
village of Whipsnade, which is visited by both walks, is notable for
the extensive green around which its scattered cottages are situated
and being the highest village in Bedfordshire. Its brick-built church
has a sixteenth-century tower and eighteenth-century nave but
incorporates some details of an earlier building, while at the back of
the village is the Tree Cathedral planted in the 1930s by E.K.Blyth
in memory of friends killed in the First World War and now looked
after by the National Trust. However what Whipsnade is best
known for is the Wild Animal Park which was opened by the Royal
Zoological Society in 1931 to exhibit its hardier animals in natural
surroundings. The Wild Animal Park in its scenically spectacular
setting can be toured by a steam railway which you may hear in the
course of your walk.

    Both walks commence by taking you along the crest of the Downs
with superb views before making for Whipsnade village, while

Walk A additionally explores the upland plateau around Studham with its pleasant mixture of woods and farmland.

Starting from Bison Hill Car Park at Whipsnade Downs, **both walks** climb a flight of steps on its east side, then turn left onto a National Trust permissive path, keeping left at a fork, ignoring a crossing bridleway and soon emerging through gates onto open downland. Now follow a right-hand hedge, later a fence straight on, wiggling to your right at one point, with panoramic views to your left including Ivinghoe Beacon, the prominent fourteenth-century Edlesborough Church on its hillock, Totternhoe Knolls, the site of a Bronze Age fort and Norman castle and later Dunstable Downs ahead. After half a mile, at the far end of Sallowspring Wood to your right, turn right following the fence of the wood to a bridlegate in a field corner. Go through this and briefly joining the Chiltern Way, take bridleway WP1 straight on along the edge of the wood, soon crossing a macadam drive and continuing beside the wood, now with a hedge to your left. On approaching a track in woodland to your right, do **not** join it but, leaving the Chiltern Way, bear slightly left into a sunken way, still following the edge of the wood, then passing through it. On leaving the wood, follow a right-hand hedge through a field, then take a sunken green lane straight on downhill, eventually ignoring a branching lane to your left and shortly emerging onto Whipsnade Green. Here follow a grassy track bearing right uphill to reach the B4540.

Having crossed the road, **Walk B** turns right and follows the B4540 verge to a sharp right.hand bend. Here cross a side-road and now read the last paragraph. For **Walk A** ignore a macadam drive to your left and take a grassy track straight on across the green to the churchyard gate. Here, briefly rejoining the Chiltern Way, take path WP8 into the churchyard, leaving the gravel path and passing right of the church then bearing half left to a kissing-gate in the back hedge. Now follow a left-hand hedge to a gate and kissing-gate, then, leaving the Chiltern Way, take path ST11 straight on beside a right-hand hedge to a kissing-gate onto Dunstable Road. On reaching a corner of Heath Wood to your right, turn right through a hedge gap onto path ST12 and follow the outside edge of the wood to the far side of the field. Here take a fenced path straight on between gardens to a road called Woodland Rise at Holywell.

Turn left onto its pavement and follow it round a bend. Just past house no.25, turn left onto a fenced path (still path ST12). Shortly before the far end of the left-hand fence, fork right onto a woodland path, soon passing the backs of a number of gardens and becoming path ST37. After a quarter mile, at a staggered path junction, turn right, then fork left onto path ST4, soon bearing right and following the inside edge of the wood uphill, later with a garden hedge to your right. On emerging into a field, follow a right-hand fence straight on, then, at the far side of the field, take a fenced path straight on along the outside edge of a wood. After some 70 yards, turn left into the wood onto winding path ST13 which takes you straight across the wood. At the far side of the wood, go straight on across a field to the near right-hand corner of a copse called Ashen Grove. Follow its outside edge straight on to the far end of the copse, then go straight on across the field, passing right of a tree to reach the corner of a hedge. Now follow this hedge straight on to the back corner of a garden, then take a fenced path straight on beside the garden to Byslips Road at Byslips.

Turn right onto this road and follow it for over 200 yards passing Hill Farm. At a double bend, turn right over a concealed stile onto path ST2 and bear slightly left across a field to the corner of a copse called Caps Grove. Here turn left and follow the edge of the copse to a stile, then bear slightly right across the next field to a handgate and stile at the corner of Bell Wood. Now go straight on through two paddocks and along a fenced path to reach Dunstable Road by the 'Bell'. Turn left onto this road, then immediately right onto path ST1, keeping right of a concrete wall and following it, soon with a hedge to your right. Where the wall ends, take the fenced path straight on, soon passing through a copse. On entering a field, turn left and follow a left-hand hedge around two sides of the field, then turn left onto path ST3, a grassy track following a right-hand hedge. At the far side of the next field, ignore a stile ahead and turn right onto path ST18 (joining Walk 17), then follow this grassy track beside a left-hand hedge. At the far side of the field take the track straight on through a hedge gap, then bearing half right (now on path ST19) to the corner of a tree-belt surrounding Studham churchyard. Here join a farm road bearing half left past the churchyard to reach a crossing track, then take path ST21 straight on over a stile, following a right-hand fence past two trees and then bearing slightly left and diverging from the fence to reach a stile and footbridge into a wood called Church Grove.

Cross these and (leaving Walk 17 and rejoining the Chiltern Way) turn right onto bridleway ST6 along the inside edge of the wood. Where this forks, go right, leaving the wood and taking a grassy track beside a right-hand hedge straight on through two fields to enter a copse. Here ignore a branching bridleway to the left and go straight on through the copse, then continue between the perimeter fence of Whipsnade Wild Animal Park and a thick hedge for a third of a mile to Studham Lane. Turn left onto this disused road and follow it

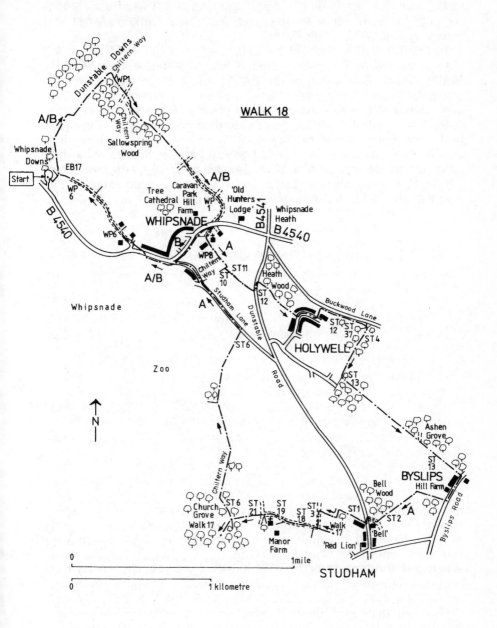

WALK 18

straight on for nearly half a mile, ignoring a left-hand fork and a footpath to your right (where you leave the Chiltern Way) and emerging onto Whipsnade Green.

Just before the junction of Studham Lane and the B4540, fork left onto a worn path along the verge of the B4540 rejoining **Walk B**. **Walks A and B** now follow the B4540 verge to the beginning of a triangular green on the other side of the road. Here cross the road and take a worn path across the rear of the green to join a macadam access road. Follow this straight on to its end, then go straight on through a bridlegate onto fenced bridleway WP6. After passing a bungalow, continue straight on, now climbing gently between hedges for a third of a mile to the top of Whipsnade Downs, where the bridleway (now EB17) begins to descend again and reaches open downland. Here bear half left to reach the steps leading down into the car park.

WALK 19:   Dunstable Downs

Length of Walk: 6.8 miles / 10.9 Km
Starting Point: Entrance to the main car park on Dunstable
Downs.
Grid Ref: TL008198
Maps: OS Landranger Sheets 165 & 166
OS Explorer Sheets 192, 193 & 181 or 182
Chiltern Society FP Maps Nos. 21 & 23
How to get there / Parking: Dunstable Downs car park, 1.5 miles
south of the town centre, may be reached from it by taking
the B489 towards Aston Clinton, then turning left onto the
B4541 towards The Downs and Whipsnade. At the top of the
hill, park in one of the right-hand car parks near a low
building with a pointed roof (the Countryside Centre and
toilet block).
Notes: Deep mud may be encountered on TT12, even in dry
weather, while heavy nettle growth may also be found in
summer, particularly on path TT23.

The Dunstable Downs, with their spectacular views along the
Chilterns to Ivinghoe Beacon and out across the Vale of Aylesbury
towards Oxfordshire and the Cotswolds, are today a real 'honeypot'
for people from Dunstable, Luton and farther afield, for picnics and
walks with superb views and convenient parking. Four thousand
years ago, these hills must also have been frequented, as at the
northern end of the Downs are the Five Knolls, five huge Neolithic
or Bronze Age burial barrows, where excavations have not only
revealed remains from this period, but also a large number of
skeletons originating from the fifth century A.D., some of whom had
injured bones or their hands tied behind their backs suggesting that
they were the victims of some battle or massacre.

Much of the walk, indeed, traverses terrain which has yielded
evidence of early settlement, as, after passing the Five Knolls, you
descend to the junction of the Ancient British Icknield Way and the
equally ancient Green Lane, before following Green Lane past the
Bronze Age camp known as Maiden Bower and modern lime pits
and continuing to Totternhoe with its Bronze Age hill fort, Norman
castle earthworks and mediæval stone pits at Lower End and the site
of a Roman villa at Church End. In addition to its historical aspects,

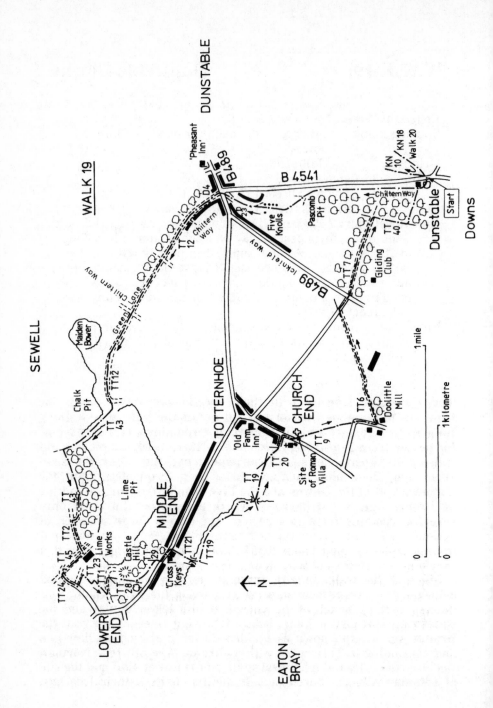

WALK 19

SEWELL

DUNSTABLE

TOTTERNHOE

MIDDLE END

LOWER END

CHURCH END

EATON BRAY

Maiden Bower

Chalk Pit

Lime Pit

Lime Works

Castle Hill

'Cross Keys'

'Old Fam Inn'

Site of Roman Villa

Doolittle Mill

Gliding Club

Pascomb Pit

Five Knolls

'Pheasant Inn'

Chiltern Way

Green Lane and Chiltern Way

Icknield Way

B489

B 489

B 4541

Dunstable Downs

Start

KN 10 / KN 18 walk 20

TT 12

TT 40

TT 17

TT 6

TT 9

TT 20

TT 19

TT 43

TT 12

TT 45

TT 24

TT 2

TT 1

TT 23

TT 7

TT 28

TT 29

TT 21

TT 19

D4

23

N

0   1 mile

0   1 kilometre

102

the walk also provides a series of fine views and visits places of flora and fauna interest and so has something to offer for everyone.

Starting from the entrance to the main macadamed car park on Dunstable Downs by the Countryside Centre and toilets, bear half right across the car park to a macadam path out of its rear right-hand corner. Where this path bears right towards the Countryside Centre, joining the Chiltern Way, leave it and keep straight on past a row benches, then along a chalky track through an overflow car park with fine views to your left towards Totternhoe Knolls and beyond. At the far end of this car park, pass its entrance and take an obvious grassy path straight on parallel to the B4541, eventually reaching a gate and bridlegate. Go through the bridlegate and keep straight on, soon joining a chalky path which merges from your left, also part of the Icknield Way long-distance path. Take this worn path straight on rounding a steep-sided combe called Pascomb Pit, where views across Dunstable open out to your right, taking the central option at a three-way fork and climbing to the summit at the end of the Downs with its superb panoramic views. Now bear slightly right, descending gently past the Five Knolls to reach a bridlegate and kissing-gate. Use either gate and follow a worn path straight on downhill, joining path D23 to reach a mown green on the edge of Dunstable. Go straight on across the green heading for the left-hand side of a roundabout at the junction of the B489 and B4541.

At the roundabout, cross the B489 (Tring Road), then bear half right, passing through a gap beside a padlocked gate into the appropriately named Green Lane (byway D4, later D-TT12). Now follow this tree-lined lane straight on for three-quarters of a mile, at first between housing estates, then leaving the town behind, ignoring a branching green lane to your left and continuing on byway TT12. On reaching a crossing green lane, leaving the Chiltern Way, keep straight on for almost another half mile, passing within 150 yards of Maiden Bower hidden by the right-hand hedge. Where the wide lane turns left through a gate, leave it and go straight on into scrubland, soon bearing right and taking path TT43 with the fence of a restored lime quarry to your left and views to your left in places across the restored quarry towards Totternhoe Knolls and towards Stanbridge ahead. After some 350 yards, you leave the quarry behind and go straight on through scrubland. Where the path eventually forks, go left (still on path TT43), climbing a chalky slope to a stile, then turn left following a left-hand fence with views to your right towards Tilsworth and Stanbridge in places. On leaving the scrub behind, go through a gate and take a raised grassy track straight on towards Totternhoe Limeworks, soon entering a sunken way and reaching a gate and stile into a green lane. Turn left into this lane (byway TT2) and follow it for some 250 yards. On nearing the limeworks, ignore a crossing track, then turn right into another green lane (byway TT45). After about 200 yards, at a junction of tracks, turn left onto byway TT24, a rough lane leading to the end of a macadam road at Totternhoe Lower End.

Take this road straight on to the limeworks gates. Here turn left onto fenced path TT23 to the right of the gates and drive, soon turning right, then left, then right again across fields to reach a safety barrier leading in a few yards to a green lane (byway TT1). Turn sharp left onto this, following it up Castle Hill. Some 50 yards before a sharp right-hand bend, turn right through a kissing-gate onto path TT28 leading into an undulating area called ´Little Hills` where Totternhoe stone, used amongst other things in the building of Windsor Castle, was excavated from the twelfth century onwards. To your left is the castle mound capped by the earthworks of a wooden Norman castle superimposed on a Bronze Age fort, while its use for defensive purposes by the Saxons is also indicated by the Saxon name of Totternhoe, which means ´look-out house hill`.

Here ignore a branching path to your right and bear slightly left across the undulating ground, passing through a deep gully to reach a rise near the bottom of the castle mound where there are fine views out across the Ouzel valley into the Vale of Aylesbury, then bear slightly right for a kissing-gate into scrubland. Go through the kissing-gate and pass through the scrub into a beechwood, then bear left, ignoring a branching path to your right and following the contours of the hill until you reach a crossing path with steps (TT29). Turn right onto this, descending steeply, ignoring a branching path to your left and eventually reaching Castle Hill Road at Totternhoe Middle End.

Cross this road and turn left along its pavement, passing the thatched, timber-framed ´Cross Keys`. At a left-hand bend, turn right onto path TT21 beside house no.181, descending between fences into a small field. Now follow its left-hand fence straight on to a footbridge. Cross this and bear half left following a left-hand hedge to cross a stile. Now turn left over a stile by a gate onto path TT19 following a left-hand hedge and stream through two fields. At the far side of tbe second field, turn left over a culvert in a hedge gap and follow a left-hand hedge and stream to a field corner. Here bear right, ignoring a footbridge to your left and follow a left-hand hedge to a footbridge and stile near a tall tree. Turn left over these and go straight on across a field to a footbridge left of a hedge gap ahead, then follow a right-hand hedge straight on. Soon after the hedge ends, turn right over a stile onto path TT20, then bear left across two fields, heading for a building with a small turret and weather vane and crossing a stile at one point, to reach a kissing-gate. Go through this, then turn left into a lane at Church End and follow it to a T-junction near Totternhoe´s fifteenth-century church built in the local stone.

Here turn right into Church Road passing the church. Just after the pavement ends, by a macadam drive, cross the road and go through a kissing-gate opposite onto path TT9, bearing half right across a field to a rail-stile. In this field, tbe site of a fourth-century Roman courtyard villa is to your left and there are fine views of tbe Dunstable Downs ahead. Now go straight on across the next field to a rail-stile and footbridge midway between two clumps of trees, then bear slightly right across a further field to the corner of a fenceline leading to a bend in Doolittle Lane. Take this road straight on, looking out for the remains of a disused wind- and watermill called Doolittle Mill partially hidden by trees ahead. At a right-hand bend just before the mill, turn left onto bridleway TT6, following a fenced track, soon skirting a right-hand belt of trees for over half a mile to reach Wellhead Road.

Turn right onto this and at a road junction, cross the B489 and take bridleway TT7, a green lane, straight on towards the Downs. At the foot of the Downs go through a bridlegate, then turn right onto path TT40 following a right-hand fence over a rise into the next dip. Here, just before reaching a bridlegate ahead, turn left onto a permissive path following a right-hand fence steeply uphill. Halfway up the hill, stop for a rest and turn round for a view across the gliding club airstrip towards Totternhoe, then continue uphill to a padlocked gate, where a gate just to your left leads you onto the open hilltop with the visitor centre and toilets and your starting point straight ahead.

WALK 20:   Dunstable

Length of Walk: 7.6 miles / 12.2 Km
Starting Point: Salvation Army chapel at junction of Icknield
Street, Bullpond Lane and Burr Street,
Dunstable.
Grid Ref: TL017216
Maps: OS Landranger Sheet 166
OS Explorer Sheets 182 & 193
Chiltern Society FP Map No.21
How to get there / Parking: From the junction of the A5, A505
and B489 in the centre of Dunstable take the B489 (West
Street) towards Aston Clinton, then take the second turning
left (Icknield Street) where a car park is on your left.

Dunstable, at the crossroads of the prehistoric Icknield Way and
Watling Street, a Roman road from Dover via London to
Holyhead, is believed to have been inhabited since the Stone Age as
archaeologists have made finds dating from various ages in close
proximity to the town. Although a Roman staging post known as
Durocobrivae was recorded, it is believed not to have been very
large and it was only in 1131, when King Henry I founded an
Augustinian priory and constructed a royal lodge known as
Kingsbury, that 'Dunestaple` (as it was then known) became a
place of any size. Originally the Priory was of vast proportions,
being 320 feet long and having transepts 150 feet wide, but the west
towers collapsed in a storm in 1222 and the transepts, central tower,
long choir and monastic buildings were at some stage demolished to
leave the present parish church with its massive Norman columns,
round arches and fifteenth-century north tower. In 1533 the Priory
was also the scene of a major historical event as it was here that
Thomas Cranmer, the then Archbishop of Canterbury, pronounced
the annulment of the marriage of Henry VIII and Catherine of
Aragon which led to the English Reformation. In the eighteenth
century, improved road communications caused Dunstable to
become an important port of call for stagecoaches and so the town´s
inns flourished, as did the local straw-hat industry, but it has only
been in the last century that the town has mushroomed into the large
industrial town it is today.

    The walk, which explores the downland around Dunstable, for

which the town is famous, first pass through the town centre before skirting the lofty ridge of Blow´s Down, which, to some extent, still separates Dunstable from its larger neighbour Luton. It then leads you across the A5 in its valley to Kensworth Church End in a quiet Chiltern hollow before following a high ridge round Kensworth Quarry to reach the top of the Dunstable Downs. From here your return route traverses a downland golf course with superb views across the town before descending to your starting point.

Starting by the Salvation Army chapel at the junction of Icknield Street, Bullpond Lane and Burr Street, take Icknield Street to the B489 (West Street) (part of the Icknield Way), then turn right and follow it to its junction with the A5 (High Street) (part of Watling Street) and the A505. Here take the A505 (Church Street) straight on past the Book Castle, the parish church and the ´Old Palace Lodge` and ´Norman King` on the site of the royal lodge of Kingsbury. At the far end of the churchyard, turn right into Priory Road, then left into St. Peters Road. Disregard one turning to the right and at a second junction, fork right into Bigthan Road then fork immediately left into a fenced alleyway which leads you to a road junction.

Here cross the major road bearing slightly right and taking path D19 virtually opposite. Where this path forks, take the right-hand option straight on towards Blow´s Down, soon passing under a pylon where you ignore a crossing track. On reaching the end of a residential road called Half Moon Lane, take path D21 straight on through a kissing-gate, then keep right of the power lines. At the far end of a row of houses to your right, fork left onto a lesser path soon joining a grassy sunken track. Just before the far end of a line of bushes to your right, fork right to join another sunken way which keeps right of the power lines, then, at a fork, bear right again to pass right of the next pylon. Now the sunken way begins to climb passing under the power lines, with wide views across the town opening out to your right. Ignore a major crossing track and keep straight on, soon joining a left-hand fence then dropping again to a kissing-gate. Here take path CA11 straight on through scrub. After some 200 yards, ignore a crossing path and go straight on through a hedge gap into a field. Now turn right and follow a right-hand hedge. After about 150 yards by a marker post, bear half left across the field to a corner of Dame Ellen´s Wood, then follow its outside edge straight on to meet a farm road. Turn right onto this (soon on path CA12) and follow its winding course for half a mile to reach Dunstable Road.

Turn left onto its left-hand footway and follow it round a long right-hand bend. Where the footway ends, cross the road and continue along its verge to a left-hand bend. Here turn right through a squeeze-stile onto path CA14 following a left-hand hedge to the far end of the field, then a right-hand hedge straight on downhill to a squeeze-stile onto the A5 opposite Lodge Farm.

Cross this road and turn left along it. After some 50 yards, turn right just before metal gates onto path KN3 passing an industrial site to cross a stile by a gate into a field. Here follow the right-hand hedge straight on uphill to a kissing-gate into a belt of trees, then turn right onto a track in the tree belt. After about 60 yards, on reaching a crossing track, turn left, **not** joining the track but passing through a hedge gap left of it. Now follow a right-hand hedge uphill and down again. At the bottom of the dip, go through a gap in the right-hand hedge and follow the other side of the hedge straight on uphill. At the top of the rise, where the hedge turns left, bear right onto path KN6 crossing the field heading just right of Kensworth Church and left of a twin-poled electricity pylon to reach a grassy track leading to Beech Road. Cross this road and take the drive to Bury Farm straight on. On reaching the former farm, at a fork, bear right following a left-hand fence then a hedge and line of trees bordering the churchyard.

By a stile into the churchyard of this church dating from around 1120, turn right onto path KN4, joining a left-hand hedge by an oak tree at the top of a rise. Now, by a tall ash tree, turn left onto path KN19 following a short green lane along the edge of a wood. On reaching a crossing track, turn right onto path KN7, still following the edge of the wood over a rise where Kensworth Quarry comes into view to your left. Now ignore a branching path to your right, then, after the path becomes enclosed by a quarry fence, follow this fence for nearly a mile, crossing the valley, bearing left, ignoring a branching path to your right and later with superb views to your right across Dunstable to Blow's Down and several ranges of hills beyond. Having passed through a kissing-gate, continue to follow the quarry fence to a signposted junction. Here turn right up a steep bank and follow tbe edge of a left-hand wood, soon with a superb view across Dunstable opening out ahead. Where the edge of the wood turns left, leave it and bear half left across open grassland to another corner of the wood where you fork left onto path D27 following the edge of the wood downhill to a corner.

Here turn left onto path D28 entering the woodland. After about 250 yards, turn right at a fork onto waymarked path KN18 and follow its winding course through the woods for a quarter mile ignoring all branching and crossing paths. At a crossways by a large tree stump, turn right onto a crossing path and follow it for 400 yards. Now, at a T-junction turn right onto a crossing path, at one point bearing left, then later passing through a squeeze-stile by a gate and eventually reaching the B4541 opposite the Dunstable Downs car park (the

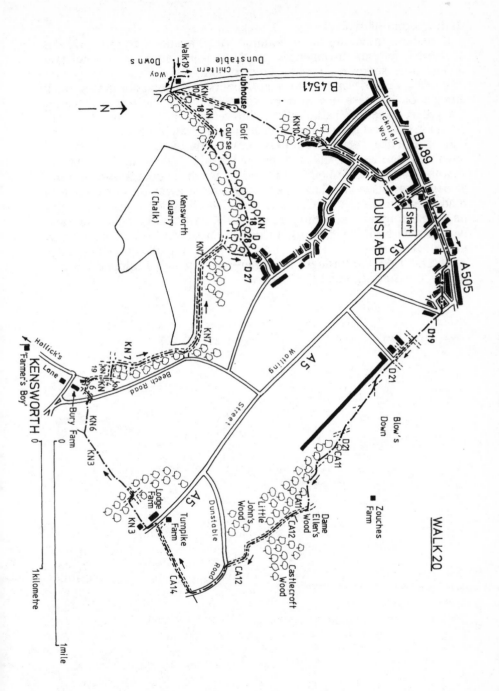

WALK 20

starting point of Walk 19).

If wishing to admire the panoramic views available from the Downs or use the public conveniences, cross the road; otherwise do **not** join it, but turn sharp right onto fenced path KN10 which leads you through a belt of scrub onto a golf course. Here take a grassy track straight on beside a line of trees with wide views ahead. On reaching the golf course car park, follow the yellow lines marking the path across it. At the far side, take a visible path straight on, aiming for the end of a hedge ahead. Here pass between the hedge and a clump of hawthorn bushes to enter a hedged path. Take this straight on downhill into and through scrubland to reach a squeeze-stile leading to a narrow macadam lane. Take this lane straight on downhill to a road junction. Here take Canesworde Road straight on for a third of a mile ignoring all branching roads. Where it finally bears left and becomes Kirby Road, turn right through the second set of green gates into a recreation ground and follow a macadam path across it to gates on the far side. Go through these then turn left into Bullpond Lane to reach your starting point.

WALK 21:   Toddington

Length of Walk: (A) 11.1 miles / 17.8 Km
                    (B) 5.5 miles / 8.8 Km
Starting Point: 'The Bell`, Toddington.
Grid Ref: TL009289
Maps: OS LandrangerSheet 166
             OS Explorer Sheet 193
             Chiltern Society FP Maps Nos. 23 & 25
How to get there / Parking: Toddington, 4.5 miles north of
    Dunstable, may be reached by leaving the M1 at Junction 12
    (Toddington) and taking the A5120 towards Toddington
    and Dunstable. On reaching the village green known as
    Market Square, turn left and park around the green. If there
    are no spaces available, take Leighton Road (signposted to
    Tebworth) opposite and park along it or in one of its side-
    streets.
Notes: Heavy nettle growth may be encountered in places in
    summer, particularly on paths TD54 and TD42.

Today Toddington is probably best known for its M1 service area,
but the village on its hilltop little more than a mile away with its
church, pubs and cottages ranged around a picturesque green
seems like a different world. In the past Toddington would seem to
have been a place of some importance as it has an old town hall and
its green is known as Market Square recalling the fact that it was
once a market town. Its cruciform thirteenth-century church was
lavishly renovated and extended in the fifteenth century when the
wool trade had made the town rich. Inside this church is the
Wentworth Chapel where Henrietta Maria Wentworth was buried
in 1686. Born at Toddington in 1657, she became mistress of the
Duke of Monmouth, first natural son of Charles II, who
unsuccessfully attempted to overthrow James II in 1685 and was
subsequently executed. Just to the east of the church is Conger Hill,
a twelfth-century flat-topped castle motte which provides superb
views across the Flit valley to a part of the Chiltern escarpment
known as the Sundon Hills. The name 'Conger` is believed to be a
corruption of 'conynger` meaning a 'rabbit warren` .
    Both walks commence by crossing the village green and passing
Conger Hill before traversing the Flit valley with wide views and

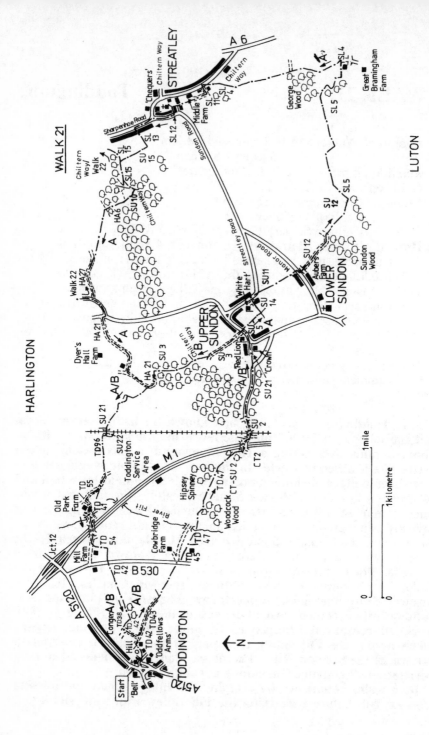

climbing the Chiltern escarpment to Upper Sundon. Walk A then explores the quiet rolling hills to the north of Luton and visits Streatley (pronounced 'Strettley`) before descending the escarpment, rejoining Walk B and returning to Toddington.

Both walks start by the 'Bell` in Toddington, crossing the A5120, passing the church and the 'Oddfellows Arms` and entering Conger Lane. Just past a white thatched cottage numbered '3`, turn left through a kissing-gate and fork half right onto path TD42 across the field, passing just right of the fenced, moated castle mound known as Conger Hill, then cross a stile and bear slightly left to a gate and stile in the far corner of the next paddock. Now turn right through gates onto bridleway TD43, taking a rough macadam track past a cemetery to your left with fine views of the Sundon Hills ahead. Now ignore a branching track to your left and continue between fences. Where the macadam surface ends, take a grassy track straight on, ignoring a fork to your left, then, where the left-hand side of the track becomes a ditch, keep right of it and follow it. Where the track and ditch bear left, leave the track and take footpath TD43 straight on across a field heading for an electricity pole right of a twin-poled pylon to reach a signposted fence gap onto the B530.

Cross this road, bearing half right and crossing a stile virtually opposite onto path TD45, passing just left of the corner of a fenced sewage works and continuing straight on (now on path TD47) to a hedge gap and raised footbridge over the River Flit. At the far end of the footbridge, turn left then immediately right across a field to the left-hand corner of Woodcock Wood. Here cross a sleeper footbridge, then turn right across the next field to reach the top corner of the wood on the skyline. Now follow a right-hand hedge straight on to the right-hand end of Hipsey Spinney, then bear slightly right through a hedge gap and follow the edge of the spinney, then a left-hand hedge to cross a stile and culvert. Here take path CT-SU2, bearing slightly right and heading for the right-hand of two hills ahead to reach the near corner of a wiggle in the hedge flanking the M1. Here go through a fence gap and take a path through scrubland to another fence gap leading to a bridge over the M1. Turn left onto bridleway CT2, crossing this bridge, then follow a concrete farm road. Where the concrete ends, bear slightly left onto the continuation of path CT-SU2, crossing a railway footbridge, then take path SU2, a sunken lane, straight on uphill. On reaching a macadam road, follow it straight on uphill between old overgrown chalk quarries for over a third of a mile. After the road levels out, where it bears right, leave it, taking path SU21 straight on between bollards into a narrow macadam lane, soon passing through a kissing-gate to reach Common

Lane at Upper Sundon. At a T-junction by the `Crown`, bear slightly left into Harlington Road and follow it to the `Red Lion`. Now **Walk A** omits the next paragraph.

Just past the `Red Lion`, **Walk B** turns left onto bridleway SU3, a gravel lane, joining the Chiltern Way and eventually reaching gates into a field. Now follow a grassy track straight on. After 350 yards, just before the gates of a sewage works, by disused gates, fork right and cross a field diagonally to a bridlegate just left of its far corner. Leaving the Chiltern Way, go through this gate and take the obvious bridleway downhill along the inside edge of scrubland for a quarter mile, eventually emerging into a field with a fine view ahead towards Harlington village on its low hill. Here turn left onto bridleway HA21, a grassy track following the left-hand hedge turning right at a corner of the field. At a waymarked junction, follow the left-hand hedge straight on, rejoining **Walk A**. Now omit the next six paragraphs.

Just past the `Red Lion`, briefly joining the Chiltern Way, **Walk A** turns right onto path SU5 along the far edge of the green, then between a pond and garden fences to a kissing-gate. Now go straight on across a recreation ground heading towards a tall pylon in the valley ahead to reach a kissing-gate in the far left-hand corner. Now, leaving the Chiltern Way, go straight on across the field to the end of a sporadic hedge, then turn left onto path SU14 along the near side of this hedge to reach a stile. Cross this, soon entering the `White Hart` car park, and take its drive straight on out to Streatley Road. Turn right onto this road, then, at a sharp left-hand bend, leave the road and take path SU11 following a right-hand hedge straight on for a third of a mile to Manor Road on the edge of Lower Sundon. Although having only a couple of farms and a few cottages, Lower Sundon can boast a large thirteenth-century church with mediæval wall paintings and stone seats around its walls for the infirm from the time before pews were provided. In the seventeenth century this church was the scene of the wedding between William Foster, a persecutor of the non-conformist preacher John Bunyan, and Anne Wingate, sister of the magistrate who had Bunyan imprisoned at Bedford Gaol.

Turn right onto this road, then, after 30 yards, turn left through a hedge gap onto path SU12 to reach a bend in a farm road. Here take the farm road straight on for a third of a mile, soon passing Sundon Wood. At the far side of the wood, where the farm road turns left, bear slightly right, soon joining and following the left side of a hedge, with views of Galley Hill, Warden Hill and part of Luton opening out ahead. On reaching a marker post, bear half left across the field, heading towards a pylon in the next field to cross a footbridge in the bottom hedge. Now turn left onto path SL5 and follow a left-hand hedge for three-quarters of a mile, at one point turning right and then left and eventually climbing to reach a corner of George Wood. Here bear half right across the field to join and follow the left side of a winding sporadic tree belt, now with closer views of Galley Hill and Warden Hill to your left. On reaching a crossing fence, turn left and follow it, later a hedge past a modern hospice.

Where the hedge bears right, turn left onto path SL4 across the field to the corner of a hedge just right of a pylon. Keep left of this hedge and follow it to a corner of George Wood, then go through a gap and follow a left-hand hedge through four fields. At the far end of the fourth field, go through a kissing-gate and bear half right across a field heading just left of a thatched cottage at Streatley to a kissing-gate just right of the end of a hedge. Here bear slightly left across the next field to cross a stile at the far side, then continue past a pond to Sharpenhoe Road at Streatley.

Joining the Chiltern Way, turn left onto this road, then immediately turn left again into Bury Lane (path SL11). Take this lane past some cottages to a gate and kissing-gate then continue to a second gate. Here turn right through a kissing-gate and follow a grassy track uphill beside a right-hand hedge. Where the track turns right into Middle Farm, leave it and take a grassy path straight on to a stile into an alleyway. On reaching the end of a cul-de-sac road, cross it and take an alleyway straight on to a gate into Streatley churchyard. The fourteenth-century church with its fifteenth-century tower has a thirteenth-century font and a mediæval wall painting of St. Catherine. In ruins for half a century, the church was thoroughly restored by Sir Albert Richardson in 1938.

Do **not** enter the churchyard, but, leaving the Chiltern Way, turn left into another alleyway (path SL12) to Sundon Road, then turn right onto its narrow footway. At a road junction, fork left onto the left-hand footway of Sharpenhoe Road, then, at the far end of the houses, turn left down some steps onto enclosed path SL13. By the gates to a radio station, go straight on through a squeeze-stile into a field and follow its right-hand hedge. After some 200 yards, turn right through a hedge gap and take fenced path SU15 to enter a wood at the far side of the field, where you join the reverse direction of Walk 22.

In the wood, rejoining the Chiltern Way, turn left onto path SL15 skirting the top of the escarpment with views through the trees to your right. On nearing a field ahead, at a fork by a flight of steps to your right, leaving the Chiltern Way, turn left then immediately right onto path SU10, entering a field and bearing half right across it to a metal gate leading back into the wood. In the wood, ignore a crossing path and take the waymarked path bearing right downhill through a storm-ravaged mature beechwood. On reaching an area of scrubby downland, where fine views open out ahead towards Harlington and

Ampthill beyond, take path HA6 straight on downhill through scrub. At the bottom edge of the scrub, ignore a crossing path and bear half left through a gate and across a field to the left-hand end of a line of trees. Here go straight on through a hedge gap, turning left onto a farm track (bridleway HA27) and continuing along it for a quarter mile to reach a road. Leaving Walk 22 again, turn left onto this road, then, at a road junction, turn right into Sundon Road and almost immediately left onto bridleway HA21 following a grassy track beside a left-hand hedge. After a third of a mile, on passing a large pond to your left, go straight on through a hedge gap, then turn right onto a grassy track passing a tree belt and farm buildings to your right. At a T-junction of tracks, turn left and follow the right-hand side of a tree belt to reach a hedge ahead where you turn right and rejoin **Walk B**.

Walks A and B now follow the hedge, soon turning right, then left then immediately left again over a bridge. Now follow winding hedged bridleway SU21 for a quarter mile. On emerging into a field near a bridge under the railway, turn left onto bridleway SU22 passing under this bridge, then turn right onto fenced bridleway TD96. By a pylon, turn right, crossing a private road and passing through a hedge gap, then bear slightly left across a field to a pylon in the middle of the field. Now go straight on towards a white house on a hillside ahead. On joining a farm track at a bend, follow its winding course (soon on bridleway TD55) for a quarter mile to Old Park Farm. Here, at a junction of tracks, turn left onto bridleway TD41, keeping left of the buildings, then bearing right to reach gates leading to a farm drive. Turn left onto this, crossing the River Flit, joining a private road which merges from the left and crossing the M1. At the far side of the motorway, ignore a branching road to the left, then, after about 50 yards, turn left onto path TD54, crossing a culvert into a field. Follow the right-hand hedge straight on for some 200 yards, then turn right over a footbridge and two stiles and follow a left-hand fence straight on to a stile and footbridge onto the B530.

Cross this road and take path TD42 straight on over a stile by a gate following a right-hand hedge to cross a stile. Now take the fenced path straight on uphill with views opening out to your left. On crossing another stile, follow the right-hand fence straight on, ignoring gates to your right, to reach a stile and footbridge into a copse. Go straight on through this, crossing another footbridge. On emerging into a field, turn right onto bridleway TD38 following a right-hand hedge then a fence to a field corner. Here turn left onto the continuation of path TD42, a fenced path along the edge of a cemetery. At the far end of the cemetery, turn right onto fenced bridleway TD43 and retrace your steps into Toddington.

WALK 22:   Harlington (Beds.)

Length of Walk: 6.0 miles / 9.7 Km
Starting Point: Harlington Village Hall car park.
Grid Ref: TL037304
Maps: OS Landranger Sheet 166
        OS Explorer Sheet 193
        Chiltern Society FP Maps Nos. 23 & 25
How to get there / Parking: Harlington, 5.5 miles north of
     Dunstable, may be reached by leaving the M1 at Junction 12
     (Toddington) and taking the A5120 towards Ampthill. After
     half a mile, at a roundabout, take a road signposted to
     Harlington Station to a crossroads in the village. Here turn
     right into Sundon Road where there is a car park by the
     village hall on your left.

Harlington, on a gault foothill of the Chilterns capped by its prominent thirteenth-century church, both catches the eye when looking out from the escarpment and provides fine views back towards the escarpment. Although the village with its station and close proximity to an M1 junction, has expanded considerably in recent years, this largely goes unnoticed when looking from the Chilterns as most of the new development is on the far side of the hill. In addition to its church, Harlington can also boast a number of attractive timber-framed and thatched cottages, but possibly its greatest claim to fame is its seventeenth-century manor house, one-time home of the magistrate Francis Wingate, who had the non-conformist preacher John Bunyan arrested at nearby Lower Samshill and brought to his house in Harlington, where he was imprisoned for the night and tried before being sent to Bedford Gaol where he wrote his ´Pilgrim´s Progress` .

     The walk, to which the view from the village positively invites you, takes you from Harlington across the valley and up the Chiltern escarpment near Streatley before leading you onto the outcrop of Sharpenhoe Clappers, with its superb views along the escarpment and out into the lowlands, descending to Sharpenhoe village and returning to Harlington.

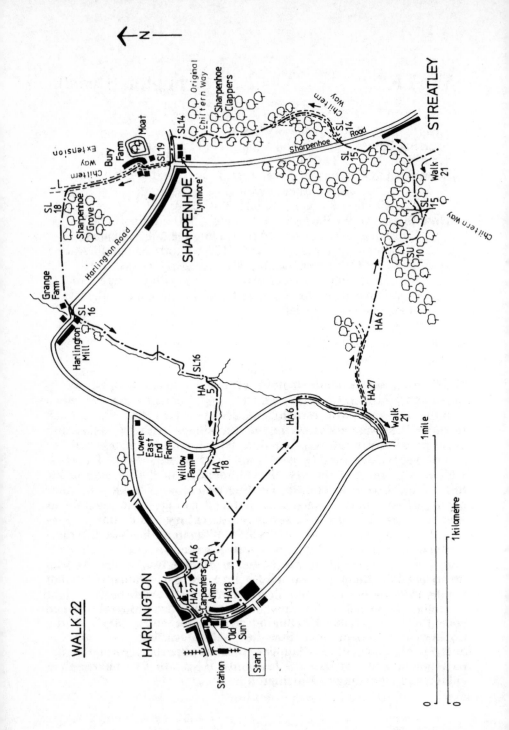

WALK 22

HARLINGTON

SHARPENHOE
'Lynmore'

STREATLEY

Station
Start
'Old Sun'
'Carpenters Arms'
HA18
HA27
HA 6

Lower East End Farm
Willow Farm
HA 18
HA 6
HA 5
SL16
HA27
HA 6
Walk 21
SU 10
SL 15
SL 15

Grange Farm
SL 16
Harlington Mill
Harlington Road

Sharpenhoe Grove
SL 18
Bury Farm
Moat
Chiltern Way Extension
SL19
SL14
Original Chiltern Way
Sharpenhoe Clappers
Sharpenhoe Road
Chiltern Way
Walk 21
SL 14
Chiltern Way

1 mile
1 kilometre
0
0

118

Starting from the car park by Harlington Village Hall opposite the 'Carpenters Arms', turn right into Sundon Road. At the village crossroads, turn right into Church Road, then, at a bend by the church, fork right onto macadam path HA27 across the recreation ground. On joining Barton Road, turn right and after some 30 yards, turn right again through a hedge gap onto path HA6, following the outside edge of a copse with fine views of the escarpment ahead. Where the copse ends, take a winding crop-break generally straight on, keeping left of a ditch when it commences. Where the ditch bears left, cross a sleeper footbridge over it, then follow the other side of the ditch, ignoring a second bridge over it by the end of a hedge and continuing along what is normally a crop break until you reach a gap in a transverse hedge and a culvert. Cross this culvert and then head for a gap in trees on the skyline until you reach a field boundary. Here bear half left, keeping right of a hedge and following it to a footbridge leading to a road.

Turn right onto this road, then, after a quarter mile at a right-hand bend, turn left through a gap by gates onto bridleway HA27, joining the reverse direction of Walk 21 and following a winding track. On reaching a left-hand plantation, where the track bears left, turn right through a hedge gap, then bear half left onto path HA6, crossing a large field with fine views of Sharpenhoe Clappers to your left to a small gate into scrubland at the top of the second rise to your left. Now ignore a crossing path and take path HA6 up some steps, then steeply uphill through scrub to an area of open downland where a seat gives you an opportunity to rest and admire the view across the lowlands behind you towards Harlington and Ampthill.

Now take path SU10 straight on uphill into mature beechwoods, ignoring a fork to your right and a crossing path, then leaving the wood by a small gate and bearing half left across a field to a hedge gap back into the wood. Inside the wood, joining the Chiltern Way, turn left, then immediately fork right and take path SL15 uphill to the top of the escarpment. Now keep straight on, soon skirting the rim of a steep-sided coombe to your left. After 300 yards, leaving Walk 21, ignore a branching path to your right and continue to follow the rim of the coombe along the inside edge of the wood, eventually crossing a stile. Now keep straight on, descending a slope, then bearing right and climbing to reach a fence where you turn left to cross a stile into a field. With fine views to your left, go straight across the field to a kissing-gate leading to steps down to Sharpenhoe Road.

Here take path SL14 straight on into a National Trust car park, passing left of a gate and following a macadam track, ignoring a crossing bridleway and continuing through a gap left of further gates. Now take a track straight on, soon climbing, then, just before the track

119

forks, turn left onto a waymarked path into woodland. Go straight on through the wood into scrubland, eventually climbing steps and joining a path which merges from your right with a superb view opening out to your left towards Toddington, Harlington and Sharpenhoe. Here keep left at a fork and take an obvious path beside a left-hand fence to reach the near left-hand corner of the mature beech copse within the ancient earthworks on Sharpenhoe Clappers known as Clappers Wood.

The name Sharpenhoe Clappers is of mixed origin, as the village name of Sharpenhoe is Saxon, meaning ´sharp spur of land`, while Clappers comes from Norman French meaning ´rabbit warren`. While the village at the foot of the hill may therefore have originated in Saxon times, the hill shows much earlier signs of habitation, as it is capped by an Iron Age hill fort and both Iron Age and Roman pottery have been found here, but the Normans adapted it for breeding rabbits and thus arose the second part of its name. Clappers Wood within the earthworks, though ancient in appearance, was, in fact, only planted between 1834 and 1844 and a painting from 1815 shows it completely bare. In the wood is an obelisk erected by W.A.Robertson in memory of his two brothers who were killed in the First World War and this was also his reason for donating the Clappers to the National Trust in 1939.

Now continue between a fence and the earthwork to the far end of Clappers Wood. Here, at a signposted fork, where the original Chiltern Way and the Chiltern Way Extension part company, take the Chiltern Way Extension straight on downhill, soon descending a long flight of steps. At the bottom you emerge into a field and follow a left-hand hedge straight on to reach Barton Road. Turn left onto this and follow it into Sharpenhoe village.

Sharpenhoe, at the foot of the Clappers, has always been a hamlet of the hilltop village of Streatley. Apart from sharing its name with the hill from which it derives, Sharpenhoe's other claim to fame is linked to the former moated manor, of which only the moat survives just to the east of Bury Farm. This house was home to both the sixteenth-century playwright Thomas Norton, a forerunner of and a model for Shakespeare and Marlowe, who was buried at Streatley in 1584 and the leading seventeenth-century mathematician, Edmund Wingate.

At a road junction by ´The Lynmore`, turn right onto bridleway SL19, the drive to Sharpenhoe Bury and Bury Farm. At Bury Farm, go through a gate, then, just past the house, wiggle slightly to your right and continue through a farmyard, passing left of some large barns onto a wide field track. After a third of a mile, on reaching a crossing power-line, leaving the Chiltern Way Extension, turn left under the power-line onto bridleway SL18, crossing a bridlebridge and then following the edge of a wood called Sharpenhoe Grove. At the far end of the wood, go straight on across the field, heading just left of a large house called Grange Farm to reach a concealed gap in the next hedge. Now keep straight on across wasteland to reach a hedge gap leading to Harlington Road.

Turn right onto this road, then after a few yards, turn left through a hedge gap onto path SL16 and follow a right-hand hedge to the far end of the field. Now follow the brook to the left for a few yards, then by a small ash tree, ignore a large footbridge with a handrail over the brook to your right and cross a sleeper footbridge by the tree into the next field. Here continue to follow the right-hand hedge for 400 yards, wiggling to your right at one point, until you reach a footbridge in the hedge. Turn right across this onto path HA5. Now turn left and follow a left-hand ditch, ignoring a footbridge across it and soon turning right. At the far end of the field, go straight on through a hedge gap and over a footbridge to reach a road.

Cross this road, pass left of the gates opposite and cross a culvert onto path HA18, then turn right and follow a right-hand ditch and hedge. At a corner of the field, go straight on through a hedge gap, then turn left and follow a left-hand hedge. Where the hedge ends, cross a footbridge and turn right onto path HA6 (temporarily rejoining your outward route) following the ditch until you reach a second footbridge across it. Ignore this footbridge and take path HA18 straight on across the field to a group of trees right of some houses on the skyline and left of the field corner. By these trees, enter a hedged path past back gardens leading to Sundon Road. Turn right onto this passing the ´Old Sun` to reach your starting point.

WALK 23:   Barton-le-Clay

Length of Walk: 7.1 miles / 11.5 Km
Starting Point: Junction of B655 (Hexton Road) & Old Road,
Barton-le-Clay.
Grid Ref: TL082306
Maps: OS Landranger Sheet 166
OS ExplorerSheet 193
Chiltern Society FP Maps Nos. 25 & 26
How to get there / Parking: Barton-le-Clay, 6 miles north of
Luton, may be reached from the town by taking the A6
towards Bedford. After about 5 miles, fork left onto the
B655 towards Hitchin. On reaching the village, turn right,
(still on the B655), then, after 200 yards, at a sharp left-hand
bend, fork right into Old Road and look for a suitable on-
street parking space.

Barton-le-Clay, formerly known as Barton-in-the-Clay, sits astride
the old route of the A6 from London to Bedford and the Northwest
of England at the foot of the Chiltern escarpment and as such, in the
days of the stagecoach, was a place of busy coaching inns. Despite
the village being swamped by modern housing from the 1960s
onwards, the vicinity of its thirteenth-century church with its
fifteenth-century tower and finely-carved roof depicting eagles,
saints and apostles, its moated sixteenth-century rectory and a
number of attractive cottages, remains an area of rural tranquillity
and beauty. For the walker, however, Barton´s principal attraction
is as a centre for walks with spectacular views of and from the
range of hills which bears its name and represents the northern-
most ridge in the Chilterns and which are thought to have been the
inspiration for John Bunyan´s ´delectable mountains` in ´Pilgrim´s
Progress`.

The walk, indeed, first takes you from Barton through arable
fields below the escarpment, offering fine views of the hills, to the
Hertfordshire village of Hexton, before climbing up a wooded
combe to explore the hilltop plateau near the Icknield Way to the
south. It then culminates by emerging at the top of a spectacular
downland combe which it skirts before descending gently back into
Barton.

Starting from the junction of the B655 (Hexton Road) and Old Road, Barton-le-Clay, take the B655 eastwards towards Hitchin. After 300 yards, turn left into Manor Road, formerly known by the intriguing name of Rogues Lane. After a third of a mile, just past house no.113 (`Oakengates`), turn right between safety barriers onto path BC2. Take this enclosed macadam path to a footbridge, then turn left with fine views of the hills to your right and follow a left-hand hedge to a field corner where you turn right. After about 70 yards, turn left through a hedge gap, then turn right onto path BC23 following a right-hand hedge straight on. Where the hedge ends, take a grassy track straight on with Shillington Church and a water tower at Upper Stondon coming into view on hilltops to your left. On reaching the end of a hedge, keep right of it, then, at its far end, follow the grassy track turning left then right. Now follow a right-hand hedge, eventually wiggling to the right, to reach a corner of the field. Here go straight on through a hedge gap and take path SH57 following a right-hand hedge to a footbridge into Hertfordshire at the far end of the field. Cross this, then bear half right onto path HX5, crossing the field diagonally to reach a road by the right-hand end of a row of bungalows at Hexton.

The village of Hexton, in a salient of Hertfordshire surrounded on three sides by Bedfordshire, has traditionally been an estate village. Before the First World War, it was almost completely rebuilt by the then Lord of the Manor, George Hodgson. Earlier owners of the Manor, Caroline Young and her French émigré husband, Joseph de Lautour, as well as adding two wings to the eighteenth-century Manor, built a new village school and village pump and also partially rebuilt the twelfth-century church. Two sides of its fifteenth-century tower, which was not rebuilt at this period, collapsed in 1947 and since then the tower has remained a ruin.

Turn right onto the road into the village and at a T-junction, turn right again, following the village street past the `Raven` and a high wall surrounding Hexton Manor to reach a crossroads by the ornate village pump. Here cross the B655 and take the Lilley road straight on. After some 200 yards, at a left-hand bend, fork right through a gap by a padlocked gate onto path HX2 and take this green lane straight on. Where its hedges end, follow the track straight on to a fork where you keep left and take a grassy track steeply uphill between woods. At the top of the hill, follow the grassy track straight on along the outside edge of the right-hand wood. At the far end of the field, go straight on through a hedge gap, then turn right, still following the outside edge of the wood. After some 80 yards, at a corner of the field, turn left and follow the left side of a hedge for a third of a mile to gates ahead leading to a road. Turn right onto this road, then, just past the end of a tree belt, turn left through white gates onto bridleway HX1, the macadam drive to Mortgrove Farm. At the farm, take the drive straight on past the buildings, then go straight on through a gap between gates and follow a right-hand fence, later a hedge, straight on for a quarter mile to the Icknield Way (byway HX8/LL23).

Turn right onto this Ancient British green road named after Boadicea's people, the Iceni, (joining the Chiltern Way Extension and the reverse direction of Walk 24) and follow it (later as bridleway SL41) for nearly half a mile towards Galley Hill, believed to be a corruption of 'Gallows Hill' as the remains of fifteenth-century gallows victims have been found in an older barrow there. Where a tree belt begins to your right, turn right onto a grassy track beside a right-hand hedge (leaving Walk 24 again) and follow it (still bridleway SL41) for two-thirds of a mile through two fields, with wide views to your left towards Luton and Streatley at the top of the first rise. On reaching a road, turn left onto it, then, after about 150 yards, turn right through a gap by a gate onto bridleway BC16, a stony track beside a right-hand hedge. Where, after a quarter mile, the hedge ends, continue to follow the track bearing slightly left across a field with views towards lowland Bedfordshire opening out ahead. At the far side of the field, ignore a branching bridleway to your right and follow the track (now path BC1) straight on for about 30 yards, then turn right through a small gate into scrubland onto path BC15 and immediately fork right onto path BC19, soon passing through a kissing-gate. Now follow a right-hand hedge straight on past the top of a steep combe, at the foot of which are Barton Springs.

At the far end of the field, leaving the Chiltern Way Extension, go straight on through a kissing-gate by a gate and turn left onto bridleway BC16, following a stony track, passing the top of another part of the combe and Ravensburgh Castle, a 22-acre Iron Age hill fort in woods half a mile to your right. At a fork, take bridleway BC26, a grassy track, straight on over the brow of the hill, then descending and swinging left round the face of the hill, at one point passing an old chalkpit and ignoring permissive paths to right and left. Where the track ends in a field, rejoining the Chiltern Way Extension, turn right and then bear left to follow a right-hand hedge, soon with a fence to your left, to reach the end of Church Road. Here turn right, then, by the church, turn left onto fenced path BC4 leading to a kissing-gate into a recreation ground. Now go straight on across the recreation ground to gates leading to Old Road where you turn right for your starting point.

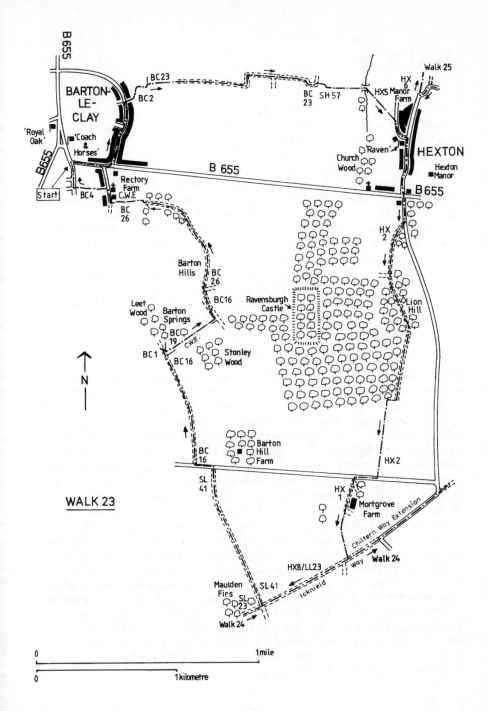

B 655

BC23
BARTON-
LE-
CLAY
BC2
BC 23   SH 57
Walk 25
HX
HX5 Manor Farm

'Royal Oak'
'Coach & Horses'
'Raven'
HEXTON
Church Wood
Hexton Manor

Start
BC4
Rectory Farm C.W.E.
BC 26
B 655
B 655
HX 2

Barton Hills
BC 26
BC16
Ravensburgh Castle
Lion Hill

Leet Wood
Barton Springs
BC 19
C.W.E.
BC 1
BC 16
Stonley Wood

N

WALK 23

BC 16
Barton Hill Farm
HX 2

SL 41
HX 1
Mortgrove Farm

Chiltern Way Extension
HX8/LL23
way
Walk 24

Maulden Firs
SL 41
SL 23
Icknield
Walk 24

0   1 mile
0   1 kilometre

125

WALK 24:   Lilley

Length of Walk: 7.5 miles / 12.1 Km
Starting Point: ʹLilley Armsʹ, Lilley.
Grid Ref: TL118265
Maps: OS Landranger Sheet 166
            OS Explorer Sheet 193
            (part only) Chiltern Society FP Maps Nos. 25 & 26
How to get there / Parking: Lilley, 3.6 miles northeast of Luton,
    may be reached from the town by taking the A505 towards
    Hitchin. 1 mile beyond the edge of the town, fork left onto a
    road signposted to Great Offley, Lilley and Kingʹs Walden.
    At a T-junction, turn left onto the Lilley and Hexton road
    and follow it for 0.4 miles into Lilley. Just past the church, at
    a right-hand bend, fork left into the continuation of West
    Street and find a suitable place to park, but do not obstruct
    driveways or use the pub car park without the landlordʹs
    permission.

**Lilley, with a large number of cottages bearing the lion rampant
crest of the Docwra (pronounced ʹDockrayʹ) and later the Sowerby
families, both of Cumbrian origin, who, at various times, owned
nearby Putteridge Bury, is clearly recognisable as an old estate
village. Its former twelfth-century church was almost entirely rebuilt
by Thomas Jekyll in 1870, but retains the Norman chancel arch
and fifteenth-century font of the original building. In the seventeenth
century, Lilley was a centre of non-conformity, being home to the
religious writer, James Janeway, and it is believed that John
Bunyan, author of ʹPilgrimʹs Progressʹ, secretly preached in the
cellar of one of the village cottages. An infamous later resident of
the village was the nineteenth-century alchemist, Johann
Kellerman, who disappeared from Lilley as suddenly as he came.**

**The walk, which includes a series of fine views, first leads you
from Lilley by way of Butterfield Green to the lofty chalk downs
and viewpoints of Warden Hill and Galley Hill near the edge of
Luton, before following the Icknield Way for 1.7 miles to near
Telegraph Hill. You then turn across a plateau called Lilley Hoo,
the site of an eighteenth-century racecourse frequented by King
George IV, before descending with fine views along and across
Lilley Bottom back into Lilley.**

Starting from the 'Lilley Arms`, take West Street back to the T-junction, then keep straight on past the church, joining the original Chiltern Way. After some 200 yards, turn right onto path LL2, entering the car park of the Cassel Memorial Hall and following its right-hand hedge into a green lane. Where this lane turns right, leave it and go straight on into a field, following its right-hand hedge (later on path LL3) past Lilleypark Wood. At the far end of the field, go straight on through a gap in the county boundary hedge and take path SL34 straight on uphill, passing just left of a single oak tree near the top and continuing to a hedge gap left of Whitehill Farm. Here cross a stile and bear slightly left towards a distant barn, crossing a field diagonally (soon on path LU26) to a stile under an ash tree leading to Butterfield Green Road.

Turn right onto this road. Where it forks, go left onto bridleway SL31, a wide farm road with extensive views opening out across Luton to your left and towards Warden Hill ahead. After passing Whitehill Wood to your right, at a crossways, go straight on for a further quarter mile. At a right-hand bend, fork left onto path SL26, following a sporadic left-hand hedge and later a line of trees, swinging left and descending. At the bottom corner of the field, turn right, soon passing through a kissing-gate into a corner of an area of scrubland on Warden Hill, then forking left onto a path into scrubland on the slopes of Warden Hill keeping the line of trees to your left. After some 300 yards, where the tall trees to your left end, by a marker post just before a flight of three steps, turn right and take ill-defined path SL28 steeply up to the top of Warden Hill, where panoramic views open out over Luton and towards the back of the Chiltern escarpment ahead.

Here go straight on, soon joining a right-hand fence and following it just below the crest of the ridge. At the far end of the ridge, go straight on through a kissing-gate, then, after 80 yards at a way-marked fork, keep right, taking a permissive section of the Chiltern Way downhill, keeping right at a second fork, to reach a kissing-gate onto fenced bridleway SL27 in a dip. Turn right onto this, then, where the left-hand fence ends, turn left, rejoining bridleway SL31 and following the left-hand fence gradually swinging left. At a corner of the field, ignore a kissing-gate and stile in the fence and turn right, still following the fence up Galley Hill, whose name is believed to be a corruption of 'Gallows Hill`, as the remains of fifteenth-century gallows victims as well as fourth-century and neolithic corpses have been found in one of the ancient barrows scattered across the hill.

On reaching a bridlegate in front of you, go through it, disregarding a branching path to your right, and continue through patchy scrub over the top of Galley Hill and one of the barrows, then descend gradually to a bridlegate leading onto a golf course. Here look to your right to check that no golfer is driving towards you, then go straight on across a fairway to a gap right of two small silver birches. Now follow a right-hand hedge straight on past a green to a gravelly track, onto which you turn left to reach a hedge gap leading to the Icknield Way. Leaving the original Chiltern Way, turn right into this ancient green lane (bridleway SL23) and follow it (later as bridleway SL41, then byway HX8/LL23) straight on for three-quarters of a mile, joining the Chiltern Way Extension and the reverse direction of Walk 23 at the first crossways, later leaving Walk 23 again and eventually emerging through a gap by a gate onto a bend in the Hexton road.

Now take this road straight on for over a quarter mile to a sharp left-hand bend. Here leave the road and take byway HX10/LL24 straight on through a gap by a gate, a disused car park and a bollarded hedge gap, then take a wide grassy section of the Icknield Way straight on towards Telegraph Hill. After a quarter mile, the Way becomes tree-lined, then, after a further quarter mile at a fork, keep right and leaving the Chiltern Way Extension, fork immediately right again onto bridleway LL9, a grassy track uphill into a copse. At the far side of the copse, continue to follow a winding grassy track uphill to reach a tumulus to your right, then take a grassy track straight on across a field at the northern end of Lilley Hoo to the corner of a hedge left of an oak tree. Here bear half right, following a winding right-hand hedge for some 350 yards. Just before a powerline, where the hedge turns right and the track forks, leave the track and bear slightly right across a large field to reach the near left-hand corner of a distant wood. Here take a grassy track straight on along the outside edge of the wood, then, at its far end, bear half left across the field, passing right of a midfield wooden pylon to join a grassy track by the corner of a hedge. Now bear slightly right and follow a left-hand hedge to enter a green lane called Lilleyhoo Lane. Take this lane straight on downhill with views towards Great Offley ahead to reach a bend in a macadam road near Lilley Hoo Farm.

Take this road straight on for 30 yards, then, rejoining the original Chiltern Way, turn right through a hedge gap onto path LL4. Now follow a right-hand hedge straight on for nearly half a mile over the top of a hill with wide views of Lilley Bottom ahead and to your left. At the far end of the field, cross a stile and bear half right across the next field, heading just right of some barns at Church Farm to a stile. Cross this and go straight across a field heading left of Lilley Church to reach the near left-hand corner of a fenced orchard, then follow the orchard fence straight on to a kissing-gate. Here continue between hedges to Lilley village street near the church, where you turn right and retrace your steps to the 'Lilley Arms'.

WALK 24

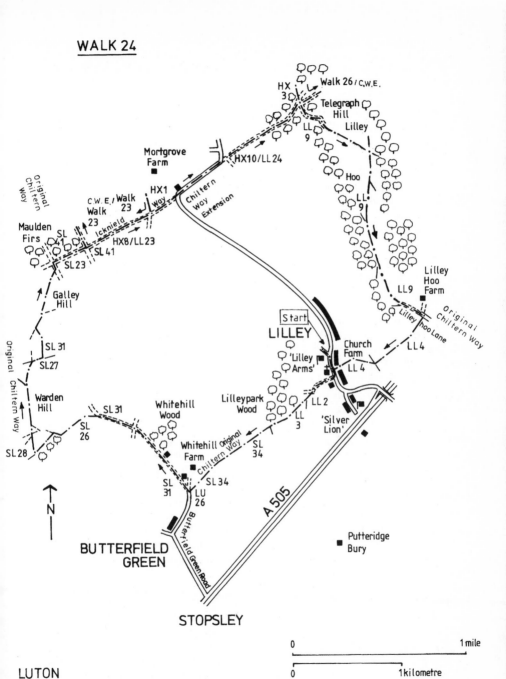

WALK 25:   Pegsdon (North)

Length of Walk: 8.0 miles / 12.9 Km
Starting Point: Entrance to cul-de-sac road at Pegsdon.
Grid Ref: TL 119303
Maps: OS Landranger Sheet 166
OS Explorer Sheet 193
Chiltern Society FP Map No.26
How to get there / Parking: Pegsdon, 4 miles west of Hitchin,
may be reached from the town by taking the B655 towards
Barton-le-Clay and following it for 4 miles, then turning
right into a road signposted to Pegsdon and Shillington.
After less than 100 yards, turn left into a wide cul-de-sac
road where you can park.

Pegsdon, a tiny village with a green and a pub at the foot of the
Chiltern escarpment below Deacon Hill, has always been a hamlet
of the Bedfordshire parish of Shillington surrounded on three sides
by Hertfordshire. In contrast, its mother village of Shillington,
which is visited in the course of this walk, with its prominent hilltop
church and a wealth of attractive brick cottages gives the
impression of having once been a place of some importance.
   The walk, by Chiltern standards one of a very easy nature for its
length, involving only one climb of any significance, keeps criss-
crossing the county boundary, first leading you along the foot of the
hills to the Hertfordshire village of Hexton. You then strike out
across the lowlands with wide views to reach the Bedfordshire
village of Shillington and its vantage point of Church Hill. From
here it continues with more wide views to the Hertfordshire village
of Pirton with its picturesque cottages and Norman church and
castle earthworks before returning over the escarpment outcrop of
Knocking Hoe with its superb views of the lowlands to Pegsdon.

Starting from the entrance to the cul-de-sac road at Pegsdon, take the
Shillington road and follow it for a quarter mile, then turn left into a
cul-de-sac road to Bury Farm and some cottages. Just past the farm,
where its macadam surface ends, take its rough continuation
(bridleway SH4) straight on, soon joining the edge of a tree belt and
bearing right. At a signposted junction at the far end of the tree belt,
turn left, still following the rough road beside the tree belt. On passing

an old watermill known as Hexton Mill, where you enter Hertfordshire, the road called Mill Lane becomes macadamed again. Now follow it for a further half mile, wiggling left at one point, then turning sharp left to reach the edge of Hexton.

At a left-hand bend about 100 yards short of the start of Hexton village, turn sharp right onto path HX6, heading for near the right-hand corner of a plantation ahead, with views of Higham Gobion's fourteenth-century church on a hilltop to your left and Shillington Church on a hilltop to your right. On reaching the plantation, follow its right-hand edge to its far end, then bear slightly right across the field, heading for a small ash tree left of a hedge, now with views of Higham Gobion Church to your left and the Chiltern escarpment behind you. By the ash tree, join a grassy track and follow it straight on beside a right-hand ditch. Where the track and ditch bear left, go straight on over a footbridge and head for the left-hand end of a hedge ahead. Here cross a footbridge at the county boundary and turn right onto path SH18, following a right-hand hedge and ditch, later a stream, to a field corner. Now turn left onto path SH19 following the right-hand hedge and stream for a further half mile through two fields. On nearing Chalkeybush Farm at Apsley End, the path bears slightly left away from the stream, soon entering a green lane and following it to cross a stile by a gate to reach Hanscombe End Road.

Cross this and take path SH20 straight on between gardens to a kissing-gate. Now follow a right-hand fence straight on through two paddocks, then pass through two kissing-gates and turn left, ignoring a third kissing-gate to your left and taking fenced path SH42 straight on beside a right-hand stream and hedge. Where the fenced path opens out into a field, bear half left onto path SH40, following a left-hand fence to a kissing-gate into a green lane (bridleway SH8). Turn right onto this, soon crossing a bridge to enter a field. Here follow the right-hand hedge straight on, soon with the wall of Shillington churchyard on your left, and climb a series of steps to reach the end of Church Street by the churchyard gate.

Shillington's early fourteenth-century stone church, with its tower rebuilt in brick in 1750 following the collapse of its old tower in 1701, is thought not to have been the first church on this hilltop site and indeed the discovery of ancient coins and Roman pottery on the hill indicates early human habitation. In any event, its elevated location suggests that in mediæval times the site will have also served a military function as a look-out post.

Now take Church Street straight on. Just past the former village school, turn right onto path SH21, a macadamed alleyway called The Twitchel, and follow it downhill to High Road. Cross this road and a footbridge, then go through a kissing-gate and follow a right-hand fence straight on across a field to a kissing-gate and culvert. Here bear slightly right, heading just right of a gap between low tree belts ahead, with Pirton Church with its `Hertfordshire spike` coming into view ahead, to reach a small culvert over a ditch. Cross this and turn right beside the ditch. In a corner of the field, turn left and follow a right-hand hedge for a quarter mile. Near the far end of the field, turn right onto path PI1, crossing the Hertfordshire boundary and entering a green lane which bears left and soon enters the corner of a right-hand field. Here go straight on, soon joining a left-hand hedge. Where this hedge turns left, leave it, bearing slightly left over the top of a rise, where a fine view opens out towards Pirton ahead and the Chiltern escarpment to your right. When Pirton Church comes into view ahead, aim just left of it to reach a culvert in a hedge gap. Here bear slightly left, heading for the near end of a hedge ahead with views towards Holwell opening out to your left. Now follow a grassy track along the left side of the hedge. Where the hedge ends and the tracks turns right, leave it and turn left across the field to the corner of a hedge, then turn right and follow the left-hand hedge round two sides of the field to reach a kissing-gate in the hedge. Turn left through it and go straight across the next field to a kissing-gate in its far left-hand corner leading to an alleyway. Go through the alleyway, then turn right into West Lane on the edge of Pirton.

Almost immediately turn left by a thatched cottage into a rough lane (still path PI1), which soon narrows to a hedged path and continues past a right-hand field before going through an alleyway to reach the end of a road called Docklands. Go straight on along the road, then, at a T-junction, turn right into Crabtree Lane and almost immediately left onto a hedged macadam path which leads to Toot Hill, then bears left to the churchyard gate.

Toot Hill to your right represents the remains of a Norman motte and bailey castle with an exceptionally large moat built by Ralph de Limesi to command the Hitchin Gap. In the light of its Saxon name, `Toot` meaning `look-out`, it is clear, however, that the Saxons must have previously had a look-out post at this point. The nearby twelfth-century church, like that of Shillington, suffered a collapse of its tower in 1874 and so the present tower dates from its reconstruction in 1876.

By the churchyard gate, turn right onto path PI16, soon passing through a kissing-gate, then take path PI17 following a right-hand fence across the meadow. Soon after the fence turns right by the corner of the moat, turn right onto worn path PI18 which leads to a kissing-gate into the end of a village street called Bury End. Follow this road bearing right, then, at a T-junction by the village green, turn

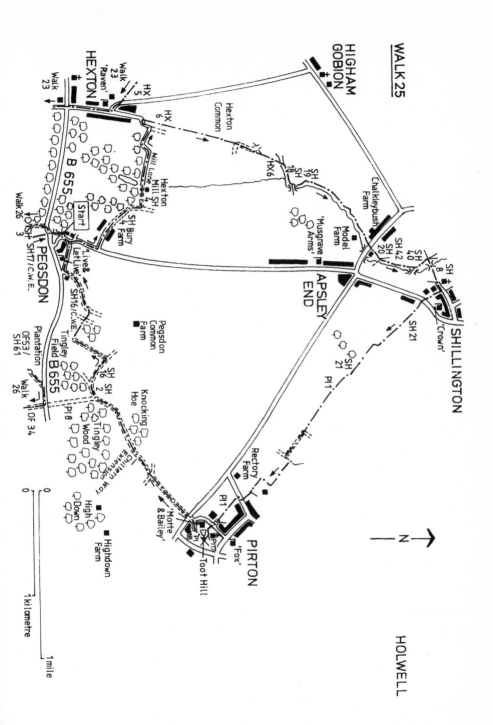

WALK 25

HIGHAM GOBION

HEXTON

Walk 23 'Raven'

Walk 23

HX 5

HX 6

Hexton Common

Mill Lane

Hexton Mill SH

B 655

Start

SH Bury 4 Farm

Chalkleybush Farm

SH 19

SH 18

HX6

Model Farm

'Musgrave Arms'

APSLEY END

SH 42

SH 40

SH 20

SH 8

'Crown'

SHILLINGTON

PEGSDON

Walk 26 3

SH7/C.W.E.

'Live & Let Live'

SH16/C.W.E.

Pegsdon Common Farm

SH 21

SH 21

Pl1

Rectory Farm

Plantation OF53/ SH61

B 655

Tingley Field

SH 16 2

Walk 26

Knocking Hoe

Tingley Wood

Pl8

Chiltern Way Extension

OF 34

High Down

Highdown Farm

'Motte & Bailey'

Pl1

Pl17

Pl9

'Fox'

Toot Hill

PIRTON

HOLWELL

N →

0

0

1 kilometre

1 mile

133

left. On reaching Hitchin Road, cross it and take hedged bridleway PI8 known as Wood Lane straight on for nearly a mile. After a third of a mile, the bridleway widens into a green road, starts to climb gently with hedge gaps giving views in places and soon joins the Chiltern Way Extension. At the top of the hill known as Knocking Hoe, by Tingley Wood to your left (a Viking name meaning 'meeting-place in a clearing`), where the lane opens out into a field and forks, turn right onto bridleway SH2, recrossing the county boundary and following a right-hand hedge. By the corner of a wood called Tingley Field Plantation, fork right through a gap by gates onto path SH16, a winding farm track down the hillside offering superb views across lowland Bedfordshire. To your right, you pass a strange-looking combe with terraces, possibly the result of chalk quarrying, backed by Knocking Hoe which is capped by a Neolithic barrow known as Knocking Knoll due to ghostly knocking sounds said to emanate from it. On reaching a crossing hedge line, turn left onto a grassy track following the right-hand side of the hedge over two rises. At the far end of the field, turn right beside a sporadic left-hand hedge bounding an old chalk quarry, soon following a left-hand fence downhill past a plantation, then descending steps to a green road. Cross this and go straight on down some steps in a hedge gap and across a field, then turn left onto a macadam farm road and follow it for a third of a mile to reach the end of Pegsdon village street near its junction with the B655. Turn right along the village street past the 'Live and Let Live`, then, at a T-junction, turn left for your starting point.

WALK 26:
Pegsdon (South)

Length of Walk: (A) 8.5 miles / 13.6 Km
              (B) 2.1 miles / 3.4 Km
              (C) 6.9 miles / 11.1 Km
Starting Points: (A/B) Entrance to cul-de-sac road at Pegsdon.
              (C)   Crossroads near ´Green Man`, Great
                    Offley.
Grid Refs: (A/B) TL119303
              (C)   TL142271
Maps: OS Landranger Sheet 166
         OS Explorer Sheet 193
         Chiltern Society FP Map No.26 (except short section of
                                             Walk C)
How to get there / Parking: (A/B) See Walk 25.
                   (C)   See Walk 27.

Pegsdon, described in Walk 25, at the foot of Deacon Hill and Telegraph Hill, with its good road access, pub and two highly scenic paths up the Chiltern escarpment, is an ideal starting point for walkers to climb and explore some of the finest and least spoilt downs in the whole Chiltern range.

Walks A and B indeed use both these paths to climb Telegraph Hill to the Icknield Way with fine views of the downs and the lowlands beneath; while Walks A and C take the Icknield Way past Deacon Hill and explore the quiet hills around Wellbury and Little Offley interspersed with further fine views across the hills and the Hitchin Gap.

Walks A and B start from the entrance to the cul-de-sac road at Pegsdon and lead you up the cul-de-sac to a right-hand bend. Here leave this road and go straight on, crossing a narrow strip of verge and the B655, then turn right onto a fenced permissive path. On reaching a tree belt, turn left through a gap by a gate onto bridleway SH3, following a fenced grassy track along the edge of the tree belt with fine views of Deacon Hill to your left and later Noon Hill ahead. After nearly two-thirds of a mile, having crossed a rise, by a corner of the left-hand field, fork right off the track through a fence gap onto fenced bridleway HX3. Now in Hertfordshire, follow it along the edge of a wood called Hoo Bit, soon with views of Galley Hill and Warden

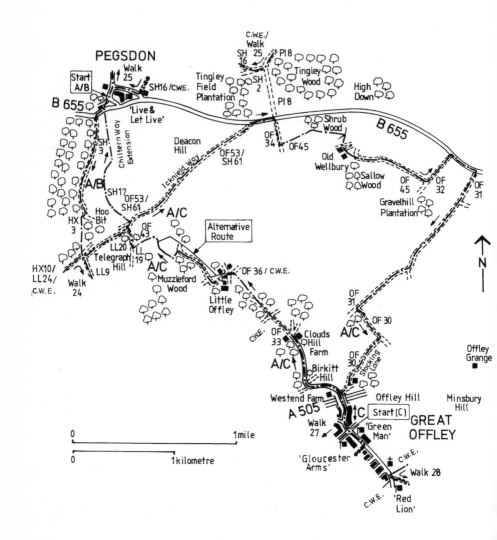

Hill near Luton to your right. At the far side of the field, go straight on through a hedge gap onto the Ancient British Icknield Way, which at this point divides into several tracks due, no doubt, to the difficulties for horse-drawn vehicles of climbing Telegraph Hill. Cross the tree-lined lower route, then, joining the Chiltern Way Extension and also briefly joining the route of Walk 24, turn left onto a parallel track, keeping left at a fork and taking a grassy track straight on up Telegraph Hill. At the top of the hill, on reaching the corner of a field known as Lilley Hoo, take the grassy track straight on along the edge of the field. At the far side of the field, joining **Walk C**, go straight on into the tree-lined Icknield Way (byway OF53/SH61).

After about 70 yards, **Walk B** turns left through a kissing-gate onto path SH17. Now read the last paragraph. **Walks A and C**, leaving the Chiltern Way Extension, follow this ancient lane along the county boundary straight on for a mile past Deacon Hill (now open access land) with the tall dense hedges eventually giving way to lower ones and the trees petering out to give attractive views of the surrounding hills and lowlands to the north in places. On reaching a gate, go through a gap beside it and a small car park and turn right onto the B655, following its generally walkable right-hand verge around a right-hand bend.

Now turn right onto bridleway OF34, following a private road. After some 250 yards, by a tall tree, turn left through a hedge gap onto path OF45 heading for a smaller tree on the skyline with a view of Tingley Wood to your left. Go straight on past this tree to reach a hedge gap at the far side of the field then continue between plantations to enter a field. Here bear half right, heading just left of two lone trees, then, by a large tree stump, bear slightly right again to reach steps down to a stile into a plantation. Follow a right-hand hedge downhill through the plantation to cross a rail-stile and the drive to Old Wellbury, then keep straight on to a stile into a field. Now bear half left uphill to the near corner of Sallow Wood. Here bear half left and take a short green lane along the edge of the wood into a field, then follow a grassy track beside a left-hand hedge straight on downhill through a large field with fine views ahead towards Hitchin and Stevenage, eventually climbing again to reach a green lane (bridleway OF32). Turn left into this lane and follow it to the B655.

Turn right onto this road, then, after some 350 yards, turn right again onto bridleway OF31. Take this green lane straight on for three-quarters of a mile, climbing gently to the top of a ridge where views of Minsbury Hill and Offley Hill open out ahead, then continuing to the bottom of the hill. Here, at a fork, go right and follow a grassy track beside a left-hand hedge. After over a third of a mile, on nearing a powerline, turn left into a branching green lane (bridleway OF30) and follow it for a quarter mile over a rise with wide views to your left. At another junction of green lanes, turn right (still on OF30) and follow this sunken way called Stocking Lane uphill for a quarter mile. On emerging into a field with views towards the lowlands over your right shoulder, follow a grassy track beside a left-hand hedge straight on through two fields to join a macadam drive. Turn right onto this and follow it to School Lane at Birkitt Hill on the edge of Great Offley. Here **Walk A** turns right, while **Walk C** turns left and follows School Lane back into the village.

Walk C starts from the crossroads near the ´Green Man` at Great Offley (described in Walk 27) and takes School Lane for a quarter mile to cross the bridge over the A505. Now **Walks A and C** follow this quiet winding road for half a mile with views to your right towards Hitchin in places. At a fork by Clouds Hill Farm, take the left-hand option, macadamed bridleway OF33, straight on towards Little Offley, with its fine late Tudor brick manor house coming into view ahead. After (re)joining the Chiltern Way Extension and entering an avenue of lime trees, at a left-hand bend, fork right off the macadam drive, following a left-hand hedge straight on. Having passed a cottage, leaving the Chiltern Way Extension, turn left onto a crossing track (bridleway OF36) into a farmyard.

Now bear slightly right off the track and across the farmyard and take a track between two black buildings ahead. (From here for the next half mile the route follows a permissive path which can be closed at any time. Should this occur, an alternative route via public rights of way is indicated on the plan, but this tends to be difficult to follow.) Follow this track straight on past the back of Little Offley House, then, at a corner of the field, turning right. Where the track forks, take the right-hand option straight on beside a left-hand hedge, later the edge of Muzzleford Wood. At the far end of the wood turn left, still following its outside edge to a field corner, then turn right and follow a left-hand hedge. Where the hedge turns left, take bridleway OF43, still following the hedge to its end. Now go straight on, soon joining a right-hand hedge and continuing beside it to a field corner. Here take bridleway LL19 straight on through a hedge gap and across a field for about 40 yards to a crossing track. Turn right onto this, now on bridleway LL20, following it into and through a copse, then beside a right-hand hedge to the Icknield Way near Telegraph Hill.

Here **Walk C** turns right onto the Icknield Way (byway OF53/SH61). Now go back five paragraphs. **Walk A** also turns right onto the Icknield Way (byway OF53/SH61), rejoining the Chiltern Way Extension and **Walk B**, then, after about 70 yards, **Walks A and B** turn left through a hedge gap and kissing-gate onto path SH17, reentering Bedfordshire. Go straight on across a field to the corner of a fence, then follow this right-hand fence straight on with views through the bushes of a deep, steep-sided combe. At a corner of the field, go straight on through a kissing-gate and bushes onto open downland, descending with views of the combe backed by Deacon Hill. Eventually you pass through another kissing-gate and follow a right-hand fence beside a belt of scrub straight on downhill with wide views. Where the scrubland ends, take a grassy track straight on over a rise, then downhill to a kissing-gate leading to the B655 opposite your starting point.

WALK 27:   Great Offley

Length of Walk: 6.8 miles / 11.0 Km
Starting Point: Crossroads near ´Green Man`, Great Offley.
Grid Ref: TL142271
Maps: OS Landranger Sheet 166
  OS Explorer Sheet 193
How to get there / Parking: Great Offley, 3 miles southwest of
  Hitchin, may be reached from the town by taking the A505
  towards Luton for 2 miles, then forking left onto a road
  signposted to Great Offley, Lilley and King´s Walden. At the
  village crossroads, turn left into the High Street and find a
  suitable parking space, but do **not** use the pub car park
  without the landlord´s permission.

Great Offley, on the old Hitchin-Luton road at the top of the
Chiltern escarpment, was formerly an important stopping point for
travellers whose horses or legs were weary from the steep climb.
Even today, although the A505 now bypasses the village, it is still
characterised by its old coaching inns. Its location also makes it an
ideal centre for walking as, not only does Great Offley give access
to the escarpment with its steep slopes and spectacular views
(explored by Walks 26 and 28), but, in addition, it offers walks in
the quiet and beautiful Chiltern uplands around Lilley Bottom and
King´s Walden. It is therefore hardly surprising that two leading
twentieth-century walkers, Don Gresswell MBE, for more than 50
years active in walking and path protection groups and founder of
the Chiltern Society´s Rights of Way Group, and Ron Pigram, well-
known author of London Transport and other walks books, chose
to live here. The village also has a long history being named after
King Offa II of Mercia, who is believed to have had a palace here
and died here in 796 A.D. In the eighteenth century, it was home to
Sir Thomas Salusbury, Judge of the High Court of Admiralty, who
rebuilt his home of Offley Place and the chancel of the parish
church (see Walk 28), where monuments to himself and other
family members are housed. His niece, Hester Thrale, who often
stayed at Offley Place as a child, also came to prominence as a
friend of Dr. Johnson.
  The walk explores the quiet upland countryside to the south of
Great Offley, crossing Lilley Bottom to the hilltop hamlets of

Mangrove Green, Cockernhoe and Tea Green, before returning by a parallel route and abounds with extensive views of the surrounding hills.

Starting from the crossroads near the ´Green Man`, take the Lilley road, soon passing the ´Gloucester Arms`. At a right-hand bend, fork left onto a side-road, ignoring Salusbury Lane to your left and taking a narrow road called Luton White Hill straight on out of the village. After a quarter mile just before a cottage, where the right-hand hedge ends permitting a fine view ahead towards Lilley, joining the Chiltern Way Extension, turn left through a gap by a padlocked gate onto path OFll, a rough track left of the cottage, and follow it beside a left-hand hedge through two fields with wide views across Lilley Bottom to your right. Near the far end of the second field, leaving the Chiltern Way Extension, ignore a branching track to your left and take path OF13 straight on beside a left-hand hedge. Soon, where the hedge and track bear right, continue to follow them past Westbury Wood through two fields and a belt of trees. Where the track turns left, leave it and go straight on across two fields, heading for an isolated house in Lilley Bottom to reach a hedge gap by a wooden pylon. Go through this gap and continue straight on to reach a road in front of the house.

Turn left onto this road, then, at the corner of the garden hedge, turn right onto path OF44 following a rough track straight on climbing gently for over three-quarters of a mile until you reach a T-junction of tracks near Mangrove Hall. Here turn right through a hedge gap and follow a left-hand fence to a field corner. Now turn left onto path OF50, joining the original Chiltern Way and following a left-hand hedge bearing left to reach a gate and kissing-gate. Go through the kissing-gate and take a fenced track then a macadam drive straight on past Mangrove Hall to reach the end of a public road by the ´King William` at Mangrove Green.

The twin hilltop hamlets of Mangrove Green and Cockernhoe with their greens and scattered cottages give a deceptively rural impression which belies the fact that both are now less than half a mile from the edge of Luton with its voracious appetite for building land. It is largely the existence of the county boundary which they have to thank for so far being spared the fate of nearby Stopsley which has long been swamped by urban development.

Take the road straight on across the green, then, after it becomes enclosed, at a right-hand bend, leaving the original Chiltern Way, fork left onto fenced path OF25, which leads you between a hedge and a fence to a stile into a field. Follow the left-hand fence across the field to cross another stile, then continue beside a left-hand hedge straight on to a rail-stile into a fenced path which leads you out to a

141

road at Cockernhoe Green. Turn left onto this road, then at a junction, turn right into Brick Kiln Lane. Follow this winding road for a quarter mile, then, on entering Brickkiln Wood, turn right over a stile by a gate onto path OF3, immediately forking left and following an obvious path flanked by hazel bushes through the wood. When you emerge from the wood, follow its outside edge, then a left-hand hedge straight on with Luton Airport and the outskirts of the town coming into view to your right. Where the hedge ends, bear slightly right across the field to the corner of a sporadic hedge, then bear half left and follow the vestiges of this hedge to the corner of a fenced plantation. Now keep straight on along a grassy track past Crouchmoor Farm to a road junction where you turn left onto the road into Tea Green.

On reaching the green, keep right at a fork passing the ᾽White Horse᾽ and continuing out of the hamlet. After a quarter mile, soon after the beginning of a left-hand hedge, turn left through a gap by a padlocked gate onto path OF23, following what is usually a crop break uphill, soon turning right, then, where the crop break ends, bearing half left across the field to reach the edge of Stubbocks Wood. Here turn right and follow its outside edge with fine views of Lilley Bottom, later passing through a hedge gap and descending into the valley. At the bottom corner of the wood, leave it and go straight on heading for the near right-hand corner of Furzen Wood to reach a hedge gap leading to the road in Lilley Bottom.

Cross this road and take path KW38 straight on through a hedge gap, following the outside edge of Furzen Wood uphill. At a corner of the field, bear slightly left to enter the wood and take a grassy track straight on through it to emerge into a rough lane. Turn left into this lane, ignoring branching tracks to left and right and later emerging into a field. At the far end of the wood, follow the track bearing right and climbing to reach a hedge at the top of the field. Here, where the track turns left, leave it and go straight on through a hedge gap, then bear half left across the corner of a field to the near corner of Judkin's Wood. Now bear half right onto a grassy track along the outside edge of the wood, soon entering it and continuing along its inside edge. On reemerging into the field, by a corner of the wood, turn left onto path KW39 following its outside edge. Where the edge of the wood turns left again, leave it and bear slightly right across a field to a hedge gap by the corner of a wood called Woodfern Wick. Here ignore a crossing track, go straight on through a gap and follow the outside edge of the wood, then, at a corner of the wood, bear half right across a field to a corner of Angel᾽s Wood. Now take path OF24 along its outside edge to pass through a hedge gap, then bear half right onto path OF12 crossing a field diagonally, heading just left of a group of

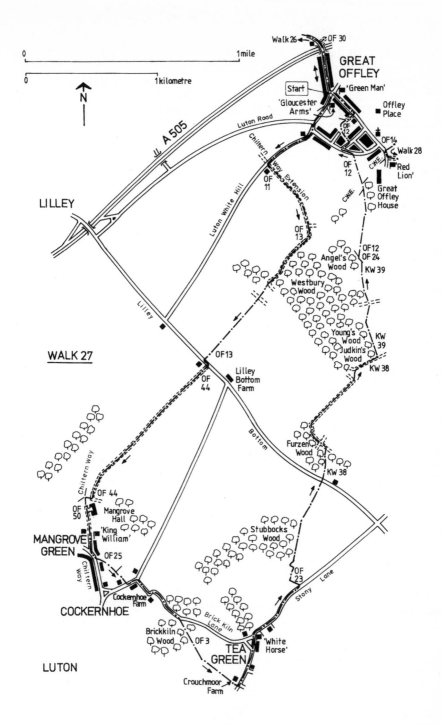

0 _____ 1mile

0 _____ 1kilometre

N

Walk 26 ← OF 30

GREAT OFFLEY

Start

'Green Man'

'Gloucester Arms'

Offley Place

A 505

Luton Road

OF 12

OF 14

Walk 28

'Red Lion'

OF 12

CWE.

CWE.

Great Offley House

LILLEY

Luton White Hill

Chiltern Way Extension

OF 11

OF 13

OF 12
OF 24

KW 39

Angel's Wood

Westbury Wood

Lilley

Young's Wood

KW 39

Judkin's Wood

WALK 27

OF 13

OF 44

Lilley Bottom Farm

KW 38

KW 38

Bottom

Furzen Wood

KW 38

Chiltern Way

OF 44

OF 50

Mangrove Hall

'King William'

Stubbocks Wood

MANGROVE GREEN

OF 25

Chiltern Way

OF 23

Stony Lane

Cockernhoe Farm

COCKERNHOE

Brick Kiln Lane

Brickkiln Wood

OF 3

'White Horse'

TEA GREEN

LUTON

Crouchmoor Farm

143

buildings around Great Offley House to reach a kissing-gate left of the far corner of the field. Go through this and follow the outside edge of a copse straight on to a further kissing-gate, then go straight on across the next field, heading towards a radio mast behind bungalows ahead, to reach a kissing-gate into Salusbury Lane on the edge of Great Offley. Turn left onto this road, then, at a junction, turn right into Gosling Avenue. Just past No. 48, turn left onto path OF12, a fenced macadam drive narrowing by garages, continuing past the end of a cul-de-sac road and crossing the village allotments. Where the path forks, bear right along a gravel access road to reach High Street, then turn left for your starting point.

WALK 28:   Hitchin

Length of Walk: 7.6 miles / 12.3 Km
Starting Point: 'The Highlander`, Upper Tilehouse Street
(A505), Hitchin.
Grid Ref: TL180290
Maps: OS Landranger Sheet 166
OS Explorer Sheet 193
(part only) Chiltern Society FP Map No.26
How to get there / Parking: From the junction of the A505 and
A602, take the A505 towards Luton for 150 yards, then by
'The Highlander`, fork right into Grays Lane and find a
suitable place to park.

Hitchin, on the River Hiz, a tributary of the Ivel and Great Ouse, at
the north-eastern extremity of the Chilterns, is probably the most
beautiful town in the whole Chiltern area. Already settled in the
Bronze Age, Hitchin and its river only derived their names in the
Anglo-Saxon period when the town became the home of the Hicce
tribe. It was, however, in the Middle Ages that the town became rich
as a centre of the wool trade which supplied the Flanders weavers.
This can be seen in St. Mary´s Church, a thirteenth-century building
lavishly remodelled by rich wool merchants in the fifteenth century.
Amongst its many treasures, this massive church contains numerous
brasses and a fifteenth-century font with a beautiful carved spire-
shaped canopy. Apart from its church, the town, the centre of which
retains its mediæval street pattern, can boast a wealth of picturesque
buildings including half-timbered houses with overhangs dating
back to the fifteenth and sixteenth centuries and therefore is well
worth exploring before or after your walk.

The walk soon leaves the town behind and leads you
southwestwards past the hamlets of Charlton, birthplace in 1813 of
Sir Henry Bessemer, inventor of an improved steel-making process,
and Wellhead at the source of the River Hiz and across the Chiltern
foothills with wide views of the escarpment before climbing the
escarpment to Great Offley. You then turn southeastwards across
the hilltop plateau to near Austage End before descending into a
peaceful combe near Offleyholes Farm, crossing further foothills
with extensive views and returning into Hitchin.

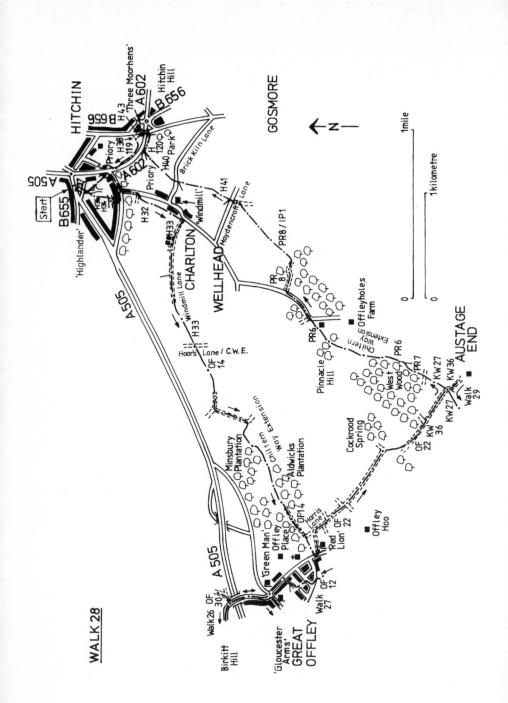

WALK 28

HITCHIN

GOSMORE

←N—

1 mile

1 kilometre

0

0

'Three Moorhens'
H43
B 656
A 602
Hitchin Hill
B 656
H38
Priory
119
H40 Park
Brick Kiln Lane
H41
A 602
A 505
Priory
H36
Start
H34
H32
H33
H33
'Highlander'
'Windmill'
Maydencroft Lane
CHARLTON
WELLHEAD
PR8/IP1
PR 8
Offleyholes Farm
Chiltern Way Extension
PR6
PR6
PR7
PR7
A 505
Windmill Lane
H33
Hoar's Lane / C.W.E.
OF 14
Pinnacle Hill
West Wood
KW27
KW36
KW27
KW36
AUSTAGE END
Walk 29
Cockrood Spring
OF 22 KW 36
Minsbury Plantation
Chiltern Way Extension
Aldwicks Plantation
OF14
Harris Lane
'Red Lion'
OF 22
Offley Hoo
'Green Man'
Offley Place
A 505
Walk 26 OF 30
Birkitt Hill
'Gloucester Arms'
GREAT OFFLEY
Walk 27 OF 12

146

Starting from the 'Highlander' in Upper Tilehouse Street, Hitchin (A505), take Russell's Slip (path H37), an alleyway along the left-hand side of the pub, to reach Wratten Road West. Cross this and turn left, then immediately right onto the continuation of Russell's Slip (path H36), walking parallel to Meadow Way at first, then continuing along an alleyway past a variety of old cottages and new houses to reach a small green, where you take path H34 straight on to steps down to Hawthorn Close. Here turn right, then immediately left, to reach Willow Lane, into which you turn left. At a left-hand bend, turn right into Charlton Road, then, at a slight left-hand bend, turn right again through white gates, then immediately left onto path H32, heading for the right-hand end of a group of trees right of a cottage, to cross a stile by a wooden shed. Now follow a left-hand fence straight on. Where the fence turns left, leave it and go straight on across a field to a hedge gap right of a group of cottages where a stile leads you out to a road at Charlton.

Do **not** join this road, but instead turn right onto bridleway H33, a rough sunken lane called Windmill Lane, and follow this gently uphill, soon with wide views of the hills to your left. Just past a cottage, where the road ends, go straight on through a gap by a gate into a wide green lane and follow it for a third of a mile. Where the lane opens into a field, follow the right-hand hedge straight on to its end, then go straight on across a field to a hedge gap by a dead tree covered in ivy.

Here cross an old green lane called Hoars Lane and joining the Chiltern Way Extension, take bridleway OF14 straight on through the hedge gap and beside a left-hand hedge for nearly half a mile. On reaching a bend in a green lane by a wooden electricity pylon, turn left into it. After nearly a quarter mile, where the lane turns left, leave it, turning right onto path OF14 and following a left-hand hedge. Where the hedge turns left, continue to follow it, eventually passing through a hedge gap by the corner of a wood called Minsbury Plantation. Now follow the outside edge of the wood straight on. At the far side of the wood, turn right through a hedge gap and bear half left across the corner of a field to the corner of a plantation. Now follow the outside edge of the plantation, later a mature wood, straight on uphill. At the top corner of the field, there is a fine view behind you across Hitchin and the lowlands to the north. Having admired this view, bear left onto a track into the wood. On leaving the wood, follow its outside edge straight on with views across the hills to your left. At the far end of the field, go straight on through a hedge gap and take a fenced path along the edge of the wood and past the churchyard to a kissing-gate onto Great Offley village street near the church and the 'Red Lion'.

The church to your right dates from the thirteenth century, but its chancel was rebuilt in about 1750 by Sir Thomas Salusbury of nearby Offley Place, a judge of the High Court of Admiralty, to display his family monuments, while the tower was rebuilt in brick in 1814. Inside are a beautiful fourteenth-century font and eighteenth-century monuments by Sir Robert Taylor and Nollekens.

Turn left onto this road, then, by the ´Red Lion`, leaving the Chiltern Way Extension, fork left into a rough lane called Harris Lane. After some 350 yards, at a sharp left-hand bend, leave the lane and take bridleway OF22 straight on following a grassy track beside a right-hand hedge. At the far side of the field at two track junctions, go straight on, taking a rough track across a large field to pass through gates at the corner of a wood called Cockrood Spring. Now bear half right across the field to a hedge gap by the right-hand end of a fence, then take a track through it, bearing left and following the hedge, later the outside edge of West Wood (now on restricted byway KW36).

At the far end of the field ignore a branching track into the wood and go straight on through a hedge gap. Now take the track straight on through two more fields. At the far end of the second field, where you briefly meet the route of Walk 29, turn left through a hedge gap onto fenced path KW27, following a right-hand hedge to the far side of the field. Here turn right through a hedge gap then immediately left through a second and take path PR7 (later joining bridleway PR6 and rejoining the Chiltern Way Extension) following the outside edge of West Wood straight on, eventually starting to descend the escarpment. On nearing the bottom corner of the field, the bridleway bears left and drops through a corner of the wood to reach a gate in the valley bottom. Go through this and keep straight on along the valley bottom, passing through a bridlegate, then following a right-hand fence to a gate into a copse. Take the obvious path straight on through the copse to a bridlegate, then follow a right-hand fence straight on across the field past Offley Holes Farm to a gate leading to a bend in a road.

Leaving the Chiltern Way Extension, take this road straight on for nearly a quarter mile passing a copse to your left. At a left-hand bend by the corner of a wood on a hillside to your right, turn right onto bridleway PR8 taking a track uphill to the corner of the wood. Here go straight on along the edge of the wood, through an outcrop of woodland, then beside a right-hand fence. Where the track drops down into the left-hand field, follow it, bearing half left to the corner of a hedge then taking bridleway PR8/IPl beside a right-hand hedge over the brow of a hill with wide views to your left at first. After nearly half a mile at a corner of the field, go straight on through a hedge gap into an ancient sunken lane called Tatmorehills Lane and turn left into it, soon reaching Maydencroft Lane.

Cross this road and take bridleway H41 straight on through a hedge gap, following a right-hand hedge, which bears left at one point, to reach a hedge gap at the far end of the field. Go through this to reach Brick Kiln Lane, then cross this road and go through a fence gap opposite into Priory Park. Now bear half right onto path H40, crossing a large parkland field to reach a marker post by the fence of the A602. Here turn right onto path H120 following the A602 fence to the end of a footbridge. Turn left over this footbridge, then at its far end, turn left through a gap in the railings onto path H43 following a left-hand fence through a copse. On reaching a kissing-gate, turn left onto fenced path H38, soon meeting and following the A602 fence. Now on path H119, follow its obvious course to join the A602 at the River Hiz bridge. Cross this bridge, then fork right onto fenced path H119, briefly rejoining the A602 verge, then forking right to reach the end of Old Charlton Road. Here turn left, soon passing through a tunnel under the A602, then forking right and continuing to the end of Wratten Close. Turn left onto this road, then, by a block of flats, fork right onto a concrete path leading to Meadow Way. Now cross this and turn right onto Russell's Slip (path H36) and retrace your steps to your starting point.

WALK 29:   Preston

Length of Walk: 7.3 miles / 11.7 Km
Starting Point: 'Red Lion`, Preston.
Grid Ref: TL180247
Maps: OS Landranger Sheet 166
OS Explorer Sheet 193
How to get there / Parking: Preston, some 2.5 miles south of
Hitchin, may be reached from the Hitchin Hill roundabout
at the junction of the A602 and B656 by taking the road
signposted to Gosmore for 2.4 miles, passing through
Gosmore and continuing straight on to Preston. At the
village green, find a suitable parking space in the side roads
around it, but do not use the pub car park without the
landlord's permission.
Notes: Heavy nettle growth may be encountered in summer,
particularly on paths KW 49 and KW34.

Preston, with its leafy green with an attractive well and pub, is the
epitome of the English village. Like most villages, it has a long
history, its manor of 'Deneslai` being listed in the Domesday Book.
In 1147 the manor was given to the Knights Templar, an order of
warrior-monks, who held it till their suppression in 1312, and thus it
became known as Temple Dinsley. The manor was subsequently
held by another monastic order called the Knights Hospitaller
before it fell to the crown in the reformation. The present house,
built in 1714 and greatly enlarged by Sir Edwin Lutyens in 1908, is
now a private girls' school. The vicinity of Preston, however, also
has other religious associations, as nearby Wain Wood was the
scene of secret midnight services with massive congregations held by
the Puritan writer and preacher John Bunyan, author of 'Pilgrim's
Progress`, while modern Castle Farm stands on the site of Hunsdon
House, whose non-conformist occupants also suffered seventeenth-
century religious persecution. This same house was converted in the
1760s to resemble a castle (hence the name of the farm) by captain
Robert Hinde, an eccentric retired army officer, whom the
contemporary author, Laurence Sterne took as the model for his
Uncle Toby in his 'Tristram Shandy`.
    The walk leads you from Preston through the quiet, rolling hill
country around King's Walden to the west, crossing Lilley Bottom

to the hilltop village of Breachwood Green, before returning by a parallel route.

Starting from the 'Red Lion' at Preston, joining the Chiltern Way Extension, take the Hitchin road. After about 120 yards, fork left into Chequers Lane. On passing a row of cottages called Chequers Cottages, turn left onto path PR4 passing between hedges to enter Church Meadow, a millennium green. Now follow its right-hand hedge straight on. At the far side of the green, go through a hedge gap and continue between a hedge and a line of fence posts to reach Butcher's Lane. Turn left onto this road and after about 35 yards, turn right through a concealed kissing-gate onto path PR5. Now bear slightly right across a field, passing right of a black wooden cowshed to reach two large hollybushes. Here bear half left, following a sporadic line of trees to a gate and stile, then bear slightly right and follow the right-hand hedge to a kissing-gate into Dead Woman's Lane (byway KW48), part of an ancient road from Hitchin to Kimpton.

Turn right into this green lane and follow it for some 300 yards. Where its left-hand hedge ends, turn left, ignoring a track to your left, and take path KW37 across a field heading just right of a black barn with a red-tiled roof at Austage End, to reach a sunken green lane by the right-hand of two holly trees. Turn left into this lane (byway KW46) and after about 120 yards, by a marker post just beyond the first right-hand oak tree, turn right onto path KW37, crossing a field to the left-hand end of a line of oaks. Here bear slightly left and follow a right-hand fence or hedge straight on until the path becomes enclosed by a left-hand hedge. Now keep straight on along a hedged path, passing left of a large new house to reach a road at Austage End.

Leaving the Chiltern Way Extension, turn left onto this road and after about 50 yards at a left-hand bend, turn right onto a grassy track (restricted byway KW36), passing through a hedge gap and bearing right to follow a right-hand hedge. At the far side of the field, follow the track wiggling to the right through a hedge gap to meet the route of Walk 28, then turn left onto path KW27 following a left-hand hedge. Where the hedge turns right, go straight on through a hedge gap and across the corner of a field to a hedge gap by the left-hand of two oak trees. Now go straight on across the next field to a hedge gap leading into a green lane. Turn right into this lane, immediately bearing left and descending to reach Stopsley Holes Farm.

Here take a track straight on between the farm buildings to the end of a road. Now follow this road straight on uphill for some 300 yards ignoring a branching road to the left. Just after a right-hand bend shaded by overhanging trees, turn left onto path KW25, a grassy track leading up into a field. On reaching the edge of the field, turn sharp right to pass through a wicket gate by a broken stile onto path KW49. Now follow this hedged path straight on for some 250 yards, crossing two stiles and eventually reaching a road. Turn left onto this road and after some 60 yards, before reaching a powerline, turn right through a hedge gap onto path KW12, bearing slightly left across a field, with wide views of Lilley Bottom opening out ahead, to reach the corner of a hedge at the left-hand end of a line of oaks. Now bear slightly right across the next field to the corner of a hedge. Here go through a hedge gap and follow a right-hand hedge downhill. At the bottom end of the field, follow the hedge turning right, then, at a corner, go straight on through the hedge into the next field. Now turn left and follow the left-hand hedge downhill to the road in Lilley Bottom.

Cross this road, bearing slightly left and take path KW33 following a left-hand hedge gently uphill. After some 200 yards, where the hedge turns left, follow it to a corner of the field, then turn right and follow the winding left-hand hedge, later a crop break. Where the crop break widens into an area of scrub, keep left of the scrub and follow its outside edge uphill with fine views of Lilley Bottom to your left and Darleyhall Windmill soon coming into view to your right. Ignore a branching path to your right, then, at the top corner of the field, go straight on into a green lane and follow it to the end of a road at The Heath, a hamlet on the edge of Breachwood Green.

Continue along this road, ignoring a branching road to the right, then, at a T-junction, take the major road straight on over a crossroads towards Breachwood Green, another village connected with John Bunyan as the pulpit he used when preaching at nearby Bendish in 1658 is housed in the village's hundred-year-old Baptist chapel. After the right-hand houses end, at a right-hand bend, turn left through a hedge gap onto path KW14, following this obvious path to a clump of bushes. Here take a grass path between fields bearing slightly right and later slightly left to enter Lord's Wood. Follow the obvious path straight on through the wood, then, at its far side, ignore a branching path to the right and follow the outside edge of the wood, later a left-hand hedge, straight on downhill to the road in Lilley Bottom.

Cross this road and a stile opposite, then bear slightly right uphill to cross a stile in a clump of trees right of the top corner of the field leading into Garden Wood. In the wood turn left onto path KW19 which soon emerges over a stile into a field. Here turn right and follow the outside edge of the wood, then, where it turns right by a tall oak, leave it and go straight on downhill and up again with glimpses of Kingswalden Bury, rebuilt in neo-Georgian style in 1972 to replace a Victorian predecessor, through the trees to your right, to reach a gate onto King's Walden village street.

152

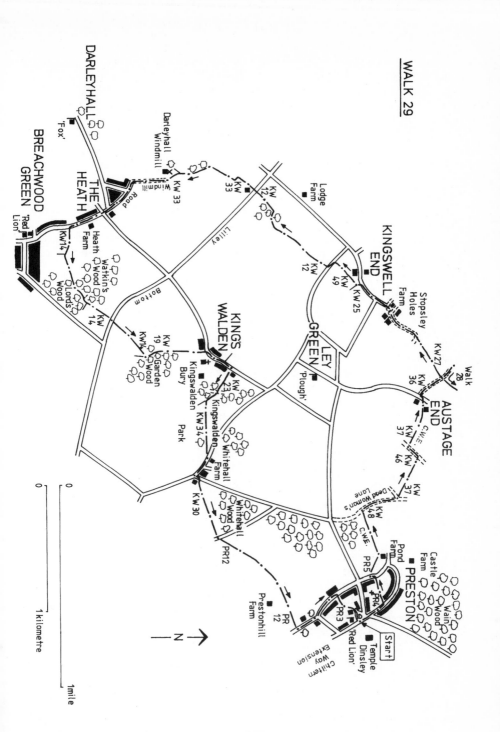

153

The name King´s Walden is derived from the village having been a royal manor in a wooded area. Its thirteenth-century church with its notable fourteenth-century painted screen and a tower from the same period contains memorials to the Hale family who lived at the Bury from 1595 to 1885.

Turn right onto the village street and follow it for nearly 300 yards passing the church and a large red-brick house, then near a black cowshed, turn right through gates onto path KW23, passing through two more gateways, then bearing slightly left across a parkland field with a clear view of Kingswalden Bury to your right at one point, to reach a kissing-gate onto a tree-lined drive. Go through this and another kissing-gate opposite, then take a worn path beside a former fenceline straight on for 140 yards. By a tall oak tree and a disused hunting gate to your left, bear half left onto path KW34 across the parkland passing right of two clumps of trees to reach a kissing-gate onto a road opposite Whitehall House.

Turn right onto this road, soon ignoring a branching road to the left, then, at a second road junction, turn left onto the Preston and Hitchin road. After some 70 yards, just past a right-hand barn, turn right through a gap by metal gates onto path KW30 into the farmyard. At the rear of the farmyard, bear half left across the field, heading for a point 60 yards right of the far right-hand corner of a wood to your left, eventually descending a steep bank to join a road. Cross this and take path PR12 through a hedge gap virtually opposite, descending several steps, then bearing half left across the field to its far left-hand corner. Here go through the left-hand of two hedge gaps and bear right following the right-hand hedge through four fields to a gate and kissing-gate leading to a road on the outskirts of Preston. Turn left onto this road, then, at a fork, go left. Just past Preston Primary School on the right, turn right onto enclosed macadam path PR3 and follow this through to a cul-de-sac lane which leads you out to the village green near the ´Red Lion`.

WALK 30:　　　　　　St. Paul´s Walden

Length of Walk: (A) 7.2 miles / 11.5 Km
　　　　　　　　　(B) 2.5 miles / 4.0 Km
　　　　　　　　　(C) 5.2 miles / 8.3 Km
Starting Point:　Southern entrance gates to St. Paul´s Walden
　　　　　　　　　churchyard.
Grid Ref:　　　TL193222
Maps:　OS Landranger Sheet 166
　　　　　OS Explorer Sheet 193
How to get there / Parking: St. Paul´s Walden, 4.3 miles south of
　　Hitchin, may be reached from the town by taking the B656
　　towards Codicote for 2.5 miles, then turning right onto the
　　B651 towards Whitwell. After 1.8 miles, at a crossroads by
　　the ´Strathmore Arms`, turn right onto a road signposted
　　to St. Paul´s Walden Church and park by the church avoiding
　　blocking field entrances. In case of difficulty, Walks A and B
　　can also be started from Whitwell, where on-street parking is
　　possible in places.
Notes: Heavy nettle growth may be encountered in summer on
　　Walks A and C, particularly on paths PW12 and LA16 and
　　bridleway LA17.

St. Paul´s Walden, set in hillside parkland overlooking the Mimram
valley in the far north-east corner of the Chilterns, is probably best
known for its disputed claim to have been the birthplace in 1900 of
the late Queen Elizabeth the Queen Mother, daughter of the Earl of
Strathmore, whose family, the Bowes-Lyons (formerly Bowes),
have owned St. Paul´s Waldenbury for more than 200 years. The
present house, which can be seen from Walks A and B, was built in
1767 and extended in 1887. The parish church, where the Queen
Mother was christened and which she attended as a child, dates
from the fourteenth century and has a chancel rebuilt by Edward
Gilbert in 1727. When this church was built, however, the village
had another name as it was then called Abbot´s Walden because the
manor belonged to St. Alban´s Abbey, but during the reformation it
passed to St. Paul´s Cathedral and so was renamed St. Paul´s
Walden in 1544. The royal wedding in 1923 did not, however,
create its first royal connection, as there is a memorial in the church
to Henry Stapleford, who died in 1631, having acted as servant to

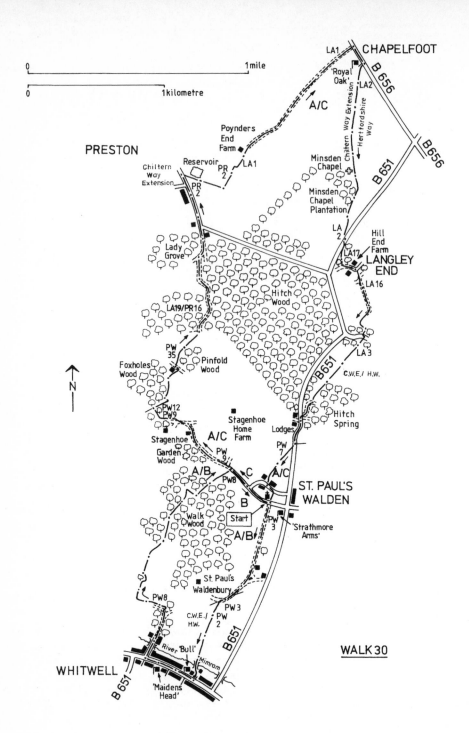

three very different monarchs: Elizabeth I, James I and Charles I. Walks A and B lead you southwards from the village through attractive parkland with fine views, to the olde worlde village of Whitwell in the picturesque Mimram valley, while Walks A and C explore the wooded hills to the north dropping to Chapelfoot in the Ippollitts valley before returning by way of the ruins of Minsden chapel and the hamlet of Langley End to St. Paul's Walden.

Starting from the southern entrance gates to St. Paul's Walden churchyard, **Walk C** turns right along the road and follows it straight on for a quarter mile to where its macadam surface ends by the site of an old lodge. Now take its stony continuation, path PW9, straight on and omit the next two paragraphs.

Walks A and B also start from these gates, but cross the road and take the fenced Chiltern Way Extension and Hertfordshire Way (path PW3) straight on, descending gently for a quarter mile through old parkland. By a cottage called The Garden House, take a tarmac drive straight on, ignoring a branching drive to the left and continuing uphill to cross an avenue of trees where you can obtain a view of St. Paul's Waldenbury to your right. On rounding a right-hand bend, fork left through a kissing-gate by a field gate, then turn left through another gate onto path PW2 following a left-hand fence across a parkland field, passing through further gates to reach a gate and kissing-gate where a view of Whitwell (pronounced 'Whittle') in the Mimram valley opens out ahead. Now take a fenced track downhill to cross a stile and farm road and reach a gate and stile leading to a footbridge over the River Mimram (until recent years often given the alternative name of Maran). Cross this bridge and bear slightly left across a field to a gate and stile, then follow a rough drive bearing right to reach the B651, Whitwell High Street, with its ancient inns and cottages.

Turn right onto this road and follow it through the village, soon leaving the Chiltern Way Extension and Hertfordshire Way. By a half-timbered cottage called The Tannery, turn right into a cul-de-sac road known as The Valley, soon recrossing the Mimram. Where its macadam surface ends, take its stony continuation straight on up a deep tree-lined sunken lane. Where the lane forks, turn left onto path PW8 to reach a gate into a field. Do **not** go through this gate, but turn right through a kissing-gate into another field, then turn left and follow a left-hand hedge. At the far end of the field, turn right and follow a left-hand hedge uphill. At the next corner, turn right again and after a few yards turn left through a kissing-gate. Now follow the left-hand hedge straight on through two fields to a kissing-gate into Walk Wood. In this wood follow a winding path straight on, soon passing a field to your left. About 150 yards beyond the far side of the field, the path turns sharp right, then, 100 yards further on, it turns sharp left. Eventually a field comes into view to your left, then keep left at a fork and continue along a narrow green lane to reach the end of a macadam road by the site of an old lodge of Stagenhoe Park where **Walk B** turns right onto the road and follows it straight on back to your starting point, while **Walk A** turns left onto the road´s stony continuation (path PW9).

Walks A and C now follow the track´s winding course past Garden Wood and an unusual Jacobean cottage to reach the macadam drive to Stagenhoe Park. Mentioned in the Domesday Book, its present house was built in 1737 and is now a Sue Ryder Home. In the 1880s it was occupied by Sir Arthur Sullivan, who composed ´The Mikado` here and outraged local people by his life-style. Turn left onto the drive (still PW9) with views of the house to your left. Where the drive forks by a white gate, fork right off it and take a grassy path beside a left-hand fence straight on to a field corner. Here continue through a hedge gap then turn right through a second hedge gap to reach a barbed-wire fence. Now turn right onto path PW12 into and through Foxholes Wood. On emerging into a field, turn left and follow the wood edge, then a garden fence, to reach a farm road by a cottage.

Turn left onto the farm road passing the cottage. By some outbuildings, turn right onto path PW35, following the outside edge of Pinfold Wood. At a corner of the wood, leave it and bear half right across a field to a hedge gap into Hitch Wood. Here take path LA19/PR16, a wide winding track between mossy banks straddling the parish boundary between Langley and Preston, straight on for over a third of a mile, later with a field visible to your left. On reaching a T-junction with another track, turn right onto it and follow it to the end of a macadam road by some cottages. Now take this road straight on to a T-junction where you turn left, soon passing Ladygrove Court and Cottages, formerly Minsden Farm.

At a road junction, (re)joining the Chiltern Way Extension, take the Gosmore and Hitchin road straight on. After 70 yards, turn right through a hedge gap onto path PR2, taking this narrow fenced path past an underground reservoir to enter a field. Now follow a right-hand hedge straight on, turning left at a field corner and continuing until you reach a stile in the hedge. Here transfer to the other side of the hedge and take path LA1, still following the hedge to Poynders End Farm with its fine wooden barns and timber-framed farmhouse. Go straight on past the farm, then take a grassy track beside a left-hand hedge. Where the hedge turns left, follow the grassy track straight on with wide views across the valley towards Hitchin to your left and Stevenage beyond the next rise. Eventually the track joins a right-hand hedge, which you follow to the B656 at Chapelfoot.

Turn right onto this road and follow it past the 'Royal Oak`, part of which dates from the seventeenth century. At the far end of the pub garden, before reaching a black wooden barn, (re)joining the Hertfordshire Way, turn right onto bridleway LA2 passing the end of the pub and turning left by a large chestnut tree into a fenced path. On emerging into a field, follow the left-hand hedge straight on gently climbing. Where the hedge ends, bear slightly left, heading just left of the ruins of Minsden Chapel to reach the corner of Minsden Chapel Plantation near the chapel ruins.

Built in the fourteenth century, Minsden Chapel was a chapel-of-ease of Hitchin parish serving the lost hamlet of 'Minlesden` referred to in the Domesday Book. By 1650 the hamlet would seem to have disappeared as the chapel was already reported to be in a decayed state and during the last recorded service at the chapel, a marriage in 1738, the curate is believed to have narrowly missed being struck by falling masonry. In the early twentieth century, the noted local historian, Reginald Hine, who was fascinated by these allegedly haunted ruins, leased them from the Church of England and was subsequently buried here in 1949.

Now follow the outside edge of the wood, later a right-hand hedge, straight on downhill. Where the hedge ends, follow the bridleway bearing slightly left then right across the field to a hedge gap leading to the B651. Turn right onto this road, then fork immediately left onto bridleway LA17 which climbs gently through hillside scrubland. On reaching a T-junction, turn left to reach the end of a macadam road by Hill End Farm at Langley End. Take this road straight on, then, at a left-hand bend, fork right onto path LA16 passing through a copse to cross a stile. Now take a grassy track beside a right-hand hedge straight on. At the far end of the field, bear right between hedges to cross a stile into a hedged path. Follow its winding course to a narrow road, then turn left onto the road and immediately right over low rails onto path LA3, heading for the right-hand end of a copse to cross a stile. Now go straight on, at first skirting the copse, then continuing ahead to join a track straight on through another copse called Hitch Spring to reach the B651.

Turn left onto this road, passing the lodge gates of Stagenhoe Park surmounted by a stag and wrought-ironwork, then, on rounding a left-hand bend, turn right through a hedge gap onto path PW7, bearing left across a field following a line of three trees to reach the corner of a hedge. Here follow the left-hand hedge straight on and on nearing a cottage, bear slightly left onto a path between a hedge and a fence leading to a narrow road at St. Paul's Walden. Turn left onto this road passing the White House, then, at a left-hand bend, fork right onto path PW3 through the churchyard to reach your starting point.

INDEX OF PLACE NAMES

Place	Walks	Place	Walks
Kingswell End	29	St. Margaret's	7
		St. Paul's Walden	30
Langley End	30	Sarratt	2/3
Latimer	2	Sewell	19
Ley Green	29	Sharpenhoe	22
Lilley	24	Shillington	25
Lilley Bottom	27/29	Startop's End	11
Little Gaddesden	13/17	Stopsley	24
Little Offley	26	Streatley (Beds.)	21/22
Little Tring	11	Studham	17/18
Lower Sundon	21		
Luton	21/24/27	Tea Green	27
		Telegraph Hill	24/26
Mangrove Green	27	Terrier's End	10
Markyate	16	The Heath	29
Marsworth	11	Toddington	21
Moor Park	1	Totternhoe	19
		Totternhoe Knolls	19
Nettleden	7	Tower Hill	5
New Mill	11	Tring	10/11
Northchurch	9	Tring Grove	11
Northchurch Common	9	Tring Reservoirs	11
Northwood	1	Trowley Bottom	15
Pegsdon	25/26	Upper Sundon	21
Piccott's End	14		
Pirton	25	Water End (Herts.)	7/14
Pitstone	12	Wellhead	28
Pitstone Hill	12	Whipsnade	18
Potten End	7/14	Whipsnade Downs	18
Preston	29/30	Whitwell	30
		Wigginton	10
Redbourn	15	Wilstone	11
Rickmansworth	1	Winkwell	6
Ringshall	13	Woodcock Hill	1

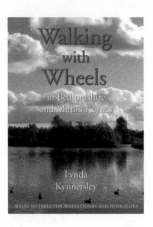

WALKING WITH WHEELS
in Bedfordshire and Milton Keynes
Walks suitable for wheelchairs and pushchairs

Lynda Kynnersley

The walks have all been chosen for their ease of access with as much information as possible about the physical features of the route, to enable people with limited mobility to decide for themselves whether a particular walk is within their ability. Some walks are on trails that have been specially adapted to make them more accessible but others are on country paths, which have reasonably flat, smooth and hard surfaces.

The walks vary in length from a mile and a half up to seven miles, with the possibility of extending them to up to fourteen miles. The majority of the walks are designed to be circular with different outward and return routes, but in a few cases there are no suitable return routes and the directions will say to retrace your steps to the start point. Details of how to get to the start point, where to park and where to find refreshments are all included, as well as general information of interest about the area and what wildlife you may see – everything in fact for a good trip out.

THE HERTFORDSHIRE WAY
A waymarked long-distance footpath

Bert Richardson

This is a walkers' guidebook to the Hertfordshire Way, a 190-mile long-distance route on public rights-of-way around Hertfordshire. The book is divided into chapters, each representing a comfortable day's walk of 11 to 15 miles. Each chapter contains a detailed description of that part of the route with a two-colour map to assist the walker, and brief notes on significant features of the landscape together with several illustrations. The book is a completely new edition of the guidebook first published in 1998 (and now out of print). All the text has been revised to take account of changes in the route, the maps have been redrawn, most of the illustrations are new, there are two new chapters covering extensions to the route, a distance chart has been included and supporting information on public transport has been updated.

The Hertfordshire Way is a fully waymarked route providing access to much of the county's very attractive countryside. Starting points for eight of the sixteen 'legs' are on main railway lines out of London, making this an easily accessible route for walkers from the capital as well as those in Hertfordshire and neighbouring counties.

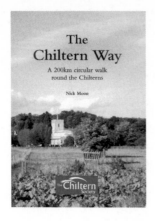

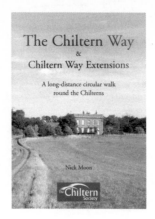

THE CHILTERN WAY
A 200km Circular walk round the Chilterns

Nick Moon

This book is a guide to the original circular long distance path through Bedfordshire, Buckinghamshire, Hertfordshire & Oxfordshire.

The Chiltern Way was established by the Chiltern Society to mark the Millennium by providing walkers in the twenty-first century with a new way of exploring the diverse, beautiful countryside which all four Chiltern counties have to offer. Based on the idea of the late Jimmy Parson's Chiltern Hundred but expanded to cover the whole Chilterns, the route has been designed by the author and has been signposted, waymarked and improved by the Society's Rights of Way Group.

In addition to a description of the route and points of interest along the way, this guide includes 29 specially drawn maps of the route indicating local pubs, car parks, railway stations and a skeleton road network and details are provided of the Ordnance Survey and Chiltern Society maps covering the route.

THE CHILTERN WAY & CHILTERN WAY EXTENSIONS
A long-distance circular walk round the Chilterns

Nick Moon

This is the new complete official guide to the now extended circular long-distance path through Bedfordshire, Buckinghamshire, Hertfordshire and Oxfordshire, whereby the society has responded to demand by incorporating further mileage both to the north and to the south of the original route.

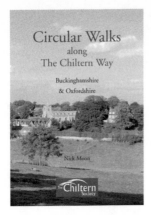
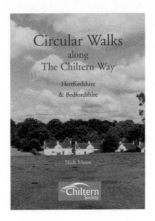

CIRCULAR WALKS ALONG THE CHILTERN WAY
Volume One   Buckinghamshire & Oxfordshire
Volume Two   Hertfordshire & Bedfordshire

Nick Moon

A two-volume series with special maps provided for each walk.

The walks range from 4.3 to 8.8 miles which makes for a comfortable half day or a leisurely full day walk. In addition, details of several possible combinations of walks of up to 22 miles are provided for those who would like a longer, more challenging walk.

Each walk gives details of nearby places of interest and is accompanied by a specially drawn map of the route which also indicates local pubs and a skeleton road network.

THE CHILTERN AREA'S LEADING SERIES OF MAPS FOR WALKERS
by Nick Moon

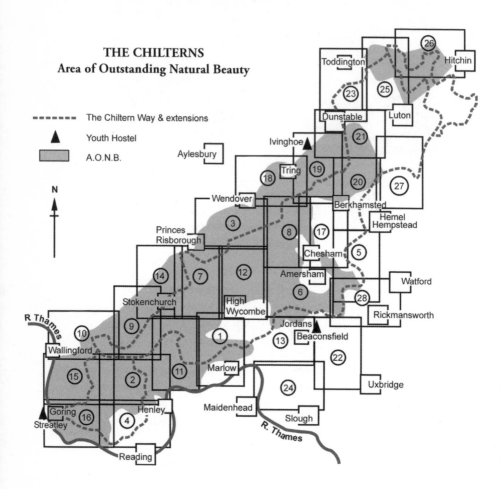

THE CHILTERNS
Area of Outstanding Natural Beauty

- - - - - - -   The Chiltern Way & extensions

▲   Youth Hostel

▓   A.O.N.B.

N

This expanding series of currently 28 maps at a scale of 2½ inches to the mile depicts footpaths, bridleways and other routes available to walkers, riders and cyclists across the Chilterns, as well as pubs, railway stations, car parking facilities and other features of interest. Several suggested walks also appear on the back of each map. New titles appear regularly and will extend coverage of the area.

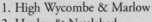

COMPLETE LIST OF CHILTERN SOCIETY FOOTPATH MAPS

1. High Wycombe & Marlow
2. Henley & Nettlebed
3. Wendover &
   Princes Risborough
4. Henley & Caversham
5. Sarratt & Chipperfield
6. Amersham & Penn Country
7. West Wycombe & Princes Risborough
8. Chartridge & Cholesbury
9. The Oxfordshire Escarpment

10. Wallingford & Watlington
11. The Hambleden Valley
12. Hughenden Valley
    & Gt.Missenden
13. Beaconsfield & District
14. Stokenchurch & Chinnor
15. Crowmarsh & Nuffield
16. Goring & Mapledurham
17. Chesham & Berkhamsted
18. Tring & Wendover
19. Ivinghoe & Ashridge

20. Hemel Hempstead & the Gade Valley
21. Dunstable Downs & Caddington
22. Gerrards Cross & Chalfont St.Peter
23. Toddington & Houghton Regis
24. Burnham Beeches & Stoke Poges
25. Sundon & the Barton Hills
26. Hitchin & Hexton
27. Flamstead & Redbourn
28. Rickmansworth & Chenies

EXPLORING HISTORY ALL AROUND

Vivienne Evans

A handbook of local history, arranged as a series of routes to cover Bedfordshire and adjoining parts of Hertfordshire and Buckinghamshire. It is organised as two books in one. There are seven thematic sections full of fascinating historical detail and anecdotes for armchair reading. Also it is a perfect source of family days out as the book is organised as circular motoring/cycling explorations, highlighting attractions and landmarks. Also included is a background history to all the major towns in the area, plus dozens of villages, which will enhance your appreciation and understanding of the history that is all around you!